ESOTE

MEDITATION

A DEFINITIVE GUIDE

by Juan Manuel Ruiz Domínguez

11 BOOKS
ESOTERIC LITERATURE

INDEX

INTRODUCTION

In an age of constant stimulation, ceaseless activity, and growing disconnection from our own inner rhythm, the practice of meditation offers a profound refuge—a return to stillness, clarity, and presence. This book was written not as an academic treatise or a fleeting collection of spiritual advice, but as a living, breathing guide for those who seek a deeper and more direct experience of themselves and the mystery of existence.

At its core, meditation is not about escaping life—it is about entering it more fully. It is not reserved for sages, monks, or mystics, nor is it limited to any singular tradition or philosophy. Rather, it is a universal human capacity to awaken to the present moment, to witness thought without being entangled in it, to feel deeply without being overwhelmed, and to see clearly without judgment.

The techniques and reflections contained in this book are drawn from a diverse range of meditative practices, woven together to form a cohesive and accessible path. You will find both foundational methods and advanced techniques, each designed to meet you where you are and invite you to explore further. Whether you are a complete beginner or a seasoned practitioner, the practices outlined here aim not only to cultivate inner peace but also to awaken transformative insight and spiritual depth.

However, this is not merely a manual for silent sitting. True meditation extends far beyond the cushion. It is a way of relating to life—a way of listening, breathing, walking, speaking, and being. The purpose of this book is to show that every moment holds the potential for awakening. Each breath, each emotion, each interaction is an opportunity to return to presence, to embody wisdom, and to live in harmony with the truth of who you are.

Throughout the chapters that follow, you'll be invited to observe the inner currents of your breath, emotions, thoughts, and energy—not to change them forcibly, but to understand them, to befriend them, and ultimately to integrate them into a greater harmony. You'll learn how the elements of nature mirror your inner world, how posture and breath unlock access to deeper states of being, and how meditation becomes not a destination, but a journey without end.

Approach this book not as something to be read once and put away, but as a companion to return to again and again. Let it challenge you, comfort you, and most of all, invite you back to the sacred simplicity of your own being.

In walking this path with sincerity, patience, and openness, you will come to see that peace is not something to be found—it is something to be remembered. And meditation is the art of remembering.

PRELIMINARIES

However, if you pause and take a moment to appreciate your partner's effort, you start a chain reaction of positivity. Your partner feels valued and carries that warmth into their interactions at work. They might compliment a colleague on a job well done, boosting their morale and productivity. That colleague, feeling uplifted, might then offer a kind word to a stranger on their commute home, brightening their day.

Ethical behavior is not just about grand gestures or significant sacrifices; it's often found in the small, everyday choices we make. Holding the door open for someone, offering a genuine smile, or listening attentively to a friend in need can all contribute to a more positive environment. These actions may seem insignificant, but they accumulate over time, creating a reservoir of goodwill that benefits everyone.

Consider a situation where you're driving home from work, and another driver cuts you off in traffic. Your initial reaction might be anger or frustration, leading you to honk your horn or make a rude gesture. This could escalate the situation, causing the other driver to react aggressively, potentially leading to a dangerous confrontation. However, if you choose to take a deep breath and let it go, you diffuse the tension. The other driver might realize their mistake and feel grateful for your patience, inspiring them to be more considerate in the future.

Forgiveness is a powerful tool in breaking the cycle of negativity. When someone wrongs us, it's natural to feel hurt or resentful. However, holding onto these feelings only harms us in the long run. By choosing to forgive, we release ourselves from the burden of anger and bitterness, allowing us to move forward with a lighter heart. This doesn't mean we condone the wrongdoing, but rather, we choose not to let it define our interactions with others.

For instance, if a friend forgets your birthday, you might feel disappointed and distant. Instead of dwelling on the oversight, you could express your feelings honestly and give them a chance to make amends. This open communication fosters understanding and strengthens your bond, turning a potential conflict into an opportunity for growth.

Empathy plays a crucial role in ethical behavior. By putting ourselves in others' shoes, we gain a deeper understanding of their motivations and challenges. This perspective can help us respond with compassion rather than judgment. For example, if a coworker seems irritable, instead of taking it personally, you might consider that they could be dealing with personal issues. Offering a listening ear or a word of encouragement can make a significant difference in their day.

Moreover, ethical behavior extends beyond our interactions with people. It also encompasses how we treat the environment and other living beings. Simple acts like recycling, conserving water, or being kind to animals contribute to a healthier planet and a more compassionate society. Choosing to buy from ethical sources, supporting fair-trade businesses, and reducing waste are all ways to align our daily choices with a more ethical lifestyle.

When we adopt an ethical perspective in our daily lives, we cultivate an inner environment that is conducive to personal growth and well-being. This ethical foundation allows us to feel better about ourselves, which in turn, makes our meditation sessions easier and more productive. The connection between ethics and meditation is profound; when we act with integrity and compassion, we create a positive emotional landscape that supports our inner journey.

Imagine starting your day with a series of ethical choices. You wake up and decide to help a neighbor by taking out their trash. At work, you go out of your way to assist a colleague with a challenging project. During lunch, you compliment the server on their excellent service. These actions, though small, accumulate and create a sense of fulfillment and purpose.

On the other hand, if you spend your day engaging in unethical behavior, such as lying to a coworker or ignoring someone in need, you carry a burden of guilt and discomfort. These negative emotions can weigh heavily on your mind, making it difficult to focus and find inner calm during meditation. The residue of unethical actions can create a barrier to spiritual growth, preventing you from experiencing the full benefits of your practice.

Ethical behavior also promotes mental clarity and emotional stability. When we act with integrity, we reduce the cognitive dissonance that arises from conflicting values and actions. This alignment between our beliefs and behaviors can lead to a more coherent and balanced mental state. For instance, if you make a conscious effort to be honest in all your interactions, you eliminate the mental strain of keeping track of lies and deceptions. This honesty can lead to a more transparent and authentic way of living, reducing stress and anxiety.

Over time, consistently choosing ethical actions rewires our minds to gravitate toward kindness, patience, and mindfulness naturally. The more we align our daily behavior with our values, the easier it becomes to meditate with a clear conscience. The energy we cultivate through positive interactions carries into our meditation, deepening our sense of peace and connection with the present moment.

In conclusion, the interconnection between ethics and meditation is undeniable. By conducting our lives with integrity, compassion, and a commitment to the greater good, we create a positive emotional landscape that supports our personal growth and spiritual development. Ethical living is not a separate pursuit from meditation; rather, it is a fundamental pillar that strengthens and enhances our practice. When we act with kindness, mindfulness, and sincerity, we naturally pave the way for deeper, more meaningful meditation experiences.

The early morning light trickled gently through half-closed curtains, casting delicate patterns across the modest apartment walls. Ava sat on the edge of her bed, her feet grounded softly on the worn carpet. Eyes closed, she breathed slowly, steadily through her nose, savoring the serenity before the rush of her day. Inhale, exhale. Each breath guided her deeper inward, anchoring her spirit amid the whirlwinds of modern life.

She opened her eyes, feeling more aligned, ready to face whatever awaited her. The aroma of fresh coffee drew her toward the kitchen, where she saw her husband, Neil, quietly pouring a steaming cup. She paused, sensing tension in his shoulders, a subtle crease between his brows.

"Morning," Ava whispered softly, placing a gentle hand on his back.

Neil smiled faintly but avoided eye contact. "Morning. I'm running late, and there's a meeting..." He trailed off, shaking his head slightly.

"Breathe," Ava said kindly, smiling as she spoke. "You've got this."

Neil took a deep breath, visibly releasing some tension, and kissed her quickly before rushing out the door. Ava watched him go, noticing the small smile he'd left behind.

On her commute, Ava noticed the impatience simmering through the faces around her, a tangible tension she had often felt herself. Today, though, she resolved to keep the calm she'd cultivated that morning. As the subway doors opened, she deliberately stepped aside, allowing a stressed-looking mother carrying a young child to exit first.

"Thank you," the woman murmured, the strain easing slightly from her face.

At her office, the quiet calm Ava carried acted as a buffer against the day's chaos. Her coworker Sarah, usually bright and *cheerful, was irritable, snapping at minor interruptions. Rather than feeling defensive, Ava waited patiently until they were alone.*

"Hey, everything alright?" she asked gently.

Sarah hesitated, eyes momentarily glistening. "I had a rough night. My brother's sick again, and I hardly slept. I'm sorry—I didn't mean to snap."

Ava placed a reassuring hand on Sarah's shoulder. "You don't need to apologize. I'm here if you need to talk or just to listen."

Sarah relaxed, her expression shifting toward gratitude. "Thanks, Ava. Really."

As the day continued, Ava witnessed small acts of negativity rippling outward. Mark, a normally friendly colleague, snapped rudely at the intern, Jason, causing the young man to retreat, wounded and withdrawn. Later, Ava approached Jason quietly, acknowledging the hurt.

"Mark's been under pressure," she explained softly. "But it's not about you. You're doing great work."

Jason's posture slowly lifted, hope and relief coloring his face. "Thanks for saying that. I was worried I messed up somehow."

When Mark later realized his harshness and approached Ava guiltily, she smiled without judgment. "It happens to all of us. Maybe talk to Jason? He looks up to you."

Mark nodded thoughtfully, recognizing an opportunity to mend the unintended damage.

After work, walking home in the amber glow of sunset, Ava reflected on the ethical currents that had run through her day. Each interaction had mattered, each moment a crossroads between fostering connection or amplifying discord. Her mindful morning had allowed her to become a positive influence, shaping her environment gently and subtly.

Arriving home, Ava found Neil already preparing dinner. He appeared relaxed, his morning anxiety long dissipated.

"How was your day?" she asked, leaning against the kitchen counter.

Neil paused, thoughtful. "Better than it started. I remembered to breathe." He smiled warmly, meeting her eyes directly.

As night fell, Ava settled once more into meditation, her breathing quiet, rhythmic, tranquil. This evening's practice flowed effortlessly, buoyed by the peace she had consciously cultivated through her day's ethical choices. Each breath felt lighter, infused with purpose and clarity.

In this quiet moment, Ava clearly perceived the interwoven threads of action and consequence, of kindness and mindfulness, forming the fabric of her daily reality. She understood, deeply and viscerally, that the tranquility of her meditation and the integrity of her actions were not merely parallel paths, but intimately interconnected, each nourishing and reinforcing the other.

Breathing quietly, Ava allowed herself to rest within that realization, grateful for the simple but profound choice of living consciously—moment by moment, breath by breath.

Healthy Habits

When we are allowed to act ethically, it is only because we are in a position where we already feel good about ourselves and the life we have. If we are constantly burdened by our own destructive habits, the task of being forgiving of others will be exponentially more difficult. Our habits shape our daily lives, influencing our moods, relationships, and overall well-being. When we engage in harmful behaviors, we not only affect ourselves but also those around us.

While it is important to have time to relax and conduct activities that could be seen as harmful, such as having a couple of beers with friends or indulging in a pizza dinner with the family, it is crucial to view them as occasional treats rather than necessities. These activities can provide temporary enjoyment and social bonding, but they should not dictate our happiness. For example, having a few glasses of wine at a social gathering can be a positive thing, enhancing the experience and fostering connections. However, requiring to drink those same glasses every day or even every week just to feel good about our lives is indeed dangerous to our well-being.

As many spiritual traditions have stated in the past, it is not enjoyment that brings suffering, but rather attachment to these forms of enjoyment. This is what addiction and dependence are like. When we become attached to certain activities or substances, we lose our freedom and become slaves to our desires. Despite smoking being a clearly unhealthy behavior, if a proud father enjoys a cigar at their daughter's wedding and completely forgets about it for the rest of his life, this unhealthy action has not become a habit and is therefore not negative on its own. The key is moderation and the ability to enjoy something without becoming dependent on it.

Ironically, activities that are often viewed as healthy, such as going to the gym or being on a diet, can become a source of attachment and suffering. For instance, if you enjoy running out in the woods but end up needing to go out every single day to feel good, you have created a negative habit out of a positive idea. The same applies to dieting; while eating healthily is beneficial, becoming obsessed with calorie counting or restricting certain foods can lead to an unhealthy relationship with food. Balance is essential in all aspects of life.

When we meditate, all these damaging habits are hindrances to our development, since they will clog our emotional system. Meditation is a practice that requires a clear and focused mind. If our minds are clouded by attachments and cravings, we will struggle to find the peace and clarity that meditation offers. After all, why meditate when all you need is a couple of beers and watching three hours of TV to achieve the same effect? The temporary relief provided by these activities is not comparable to the long-term benefits of a consistent meditation practice.

For this reason, it is important to balance our habits in a way that our lives are socially and personally enjoyable but we do not fall into the abyss of addiction and dependence. We must cultivate a lifestyle that promotes both physical and mental health, allowing us to engage in social activities without becoming dependent on them. This balance enables us to lead fulfilling lives, where we can enjoy the company of others, indulge in occasional treats, and maintain a healthy mind and body.

Creating awareness of our habits and their impact on our lives is a key step in this process. When we consciously observe our behaviors, we begin to understand which ones contribute to our well-being and which ones hinder it. This awareness, combined with the discipline cultivated through meditation, allows us to gradually shift toward a more balanced and fulfilling lifestyle. It is not about strict self-denial, but rather about cultivating habits that support our long-term happiness and peace of mind.

In conclusion, healthy habits are not just about what we do but also about how we do it. It is about finding a balance between enjoyment and moderation, between social activities and personal well-being. By cultivating this balance, we can lead happier, healthier lives, free from the chains of addiction and dependence. Through self-awareness and mindful choices, we create a life where happiness comes not from fleeting pleasures, but from a deep and lasting sense of peace.

Ethan sat quietly at his kitchen table, his fingers wrapped around a steaming cup of herbal tea, the fragrance of chamomile and lavender mingling gently in the early evening air. Through his window, the amber hues of sunset draped over the neighborhood, bathing everything in warmth and serenity. But Ethan's mind wandered restlessly, unsettled despite the tranquil scene.

His phone buzzed softly, pulling him back. The message was from Lucas, an old friend he'd known since college. "Join us tonight? Drinks and wings, usual spot!" Ethan stared thoughtfully at the screen, an internal debate rising inside him. It was Friday, after all; he deserved to relax. Yet something tugged at his conscience—a quiet voice reminding him of recent mornings clouded by hangovers and days blurred by fatigue and regret.

Taking a deep breath, Ethan typed back slowly: "Think I'll skip tonight. Catch you next time?" He set the phone down gently, feeling a subtle yet powerful shift inside himself. It wasn't denial or deprivation he felt, but rather the surprising ease of choosing balance.

Ethan had recently begun meditating—just five minutes at first, slowly building to longer sessions—and the practice had quietly begun reshaping his perspective. He now noticed things previously hidden in the chaos of daily life, like how certain habits fed an insatiable cycle of temporary pleasures that rarely translated into lasting happiness.

As the evening deepened, he decided to take a walk. The city streets buzzed with the Friday night pulse of laughter, music, and vibrant energy. Ethan smiled to himself, savoring his newfound ability to enjoy the world without desperately needing to lose himself in it.

Passing a familiar pub, Ethan glimpsed his friends inside, laughing loudly around pitchers of beer and overflowing plates. His chest tightened slightly, a fleeting sense of longing surging through him, but it quickly faded. Ethan reminded himself it wasn't about abandoning enjoyment but rather learning to savor it without dependency.

His path took him to a quiet neighborhood park. He paused at the entrance, inhaling the scent of freshly cut grass. Under a lamppost, an older woman sat calmly, eyes closed, breathing steadily. Ethan recognized her from the neighborhood—Margaret, always serene, always composed.

"Good evening, Margaret," he greeted softly, approaching with a respectful distance.

She opened her eyes, smiling warmly. "Ethan, good to see you. Taking a moment for yourself tonight?"

"Trying to," he admitted, sitting beside her. "It's strange how choosing healthy habits can feel isolating at first. Did you ever experience that?"

Margaret chuckled knowingly. "At first, absolutely. I remember struggling between wanting to feel good immediately and wanting to feel good consistently. It took years to realize those weren't always the same thing."

Ethan nodded thoughtfully. "I've started noticing how easy it is to turn healthy habits into obsessions too. I ran every morning last year until missing one day ruined my mood. It was supposed to help, not become another burden."

Margaret smiled knowingly, her gaze gentle yet penetrating. "Balance, Ethan. Every choice we make shapes us—either chaining us or freeing us. True health comes from moderation, not extremes."

Ethan leaned back, breathing in deeply. "Moderation feels elusive sometimes. Like tonight, I almost went drinking again, but said no. It felt good, yet a part of me wondered if I was becoming rigid."

"Awareness is your ally," Margaret reassured him softly. "You chose freely tonight, neither bound by cravings nor fearfully avoiding life. That's true moderation."

As they sat in quiet companionship beneath the lamppost, Ethan's anxiety faded into a profound calm. He sensed clearly the delicate equilibrium between enjoying life's pleasures and respecting his own well-being.

Over the following weeks, Ethan explored this delicate balance consciously, learning to savor life's offerings without becoming enslaved by them. He drank occasionally with friends, savoring laughter without regret. He enjoyed pizza nights with family, free from guilt. Yet, he prioritized his meditation practice, cultivating clarity and emotional health.

Slowly, Ethan's relationships deepened. His friends noticed the changes—not just sobriety, but genuine presence and attention. Conversations became richer, laughter more meaningful. At work, his patience and clear-headedness earned respect from colleagues, creating harmony rather than conflict.

Months later, sitting once more in the quiet park beside Margaret, Ethan shared his progress. "Habits shape everything," he reflected softly. "I used to chase happiness by escaping discomfort. Now, happiness finds me naturally because I've stopped running away."

Margaret smiled warmly. "It seems you've found true freedom. You've learned to master your habits rather than be mastered by them."

Ethan nodded deeply, the sunset casting warm hues across his peaceful expression. "And it's strange—now that I'm not bound to anything, I can enjoy everything more deeply."

Together, they sat quietly, breathing steadily, each aware of their own journey toward balance, clarity, and lasting peace.

Time and Setting

Finding the right moment and place to meditate is just as much of a challenge as behaving ethically and getting rid of negative habits. Both of these concepts are meant to be a support for our meditation, not replace them. Some people lead good and healthy lives, yet do not meditate. They might not feel the need for it or simply consider they have no further time available. For this reason, time and setting is the third and final support column of our meditation endeavor.

Meditation is a practice that requires dedication and consistency, but it should not feel like a burden. Some people believe meditation is some kind of full-time job. While to some it could be (nuns, monks, or meditation experts), generally it is not a requirement to get the most benefits out of this practice. Even just thirty minutes per day is enough to bring most of the benefits of casual meditation. As the practitioner starts realizing the many advantages of this habit, more time will be dedicated spontaneously. Soon, hours of TV time will feel tedious and boring compared to spending an hour meditating.

The moment of the day that someone chooses to meditate depends on our particular needs and lifestyle. Some might choose the morning, before the rest of the family is awake. Others might feel the later evening is a better choice since it is a naturally silent moment of the day. In any case, fitting a meditation session into our busy schedules must be a personal choice that does not seem like a chore. Meditation must be a moment of relaxation and enjoyment we decide to give ourselves, not a task that must be performed.

The place we choose to meditate is equally important. It is of capital importance that this place is calm, silent, and lacking any unnecessary distractions. It could be a personal room with calm music in the background where we simply sit on a carpet or yoga mat. It could be an empty spot in the forest that feels warm and safe. Any place can be a good choice if it resonates positively within us. The only core requirement is that it is a safe place without distractions.

Creating a dedicated meditation space can enhance your practice significantly. This space should be free from clutter and distractions, allowing you to focus entirely on your meditation. You can personalize this space with items that bring you peace and tranquility, such as candles, incense, or inspirational quotes. The environment should be comfortable, with appropriate lighting and temperature, to ensure you can relax fully. A comfortable cushion or chair can also support proper posture, reducing the chances of physical discomfort interrupting your meditation.

Some practitioners find that incorporating elements of nature, such as houseplants, a small indoor fountain, or natural light, can deepen their sense of calm. If meditating indoors is not always an option, consider using noise-canceling headphones or a white noise machine to block out disturbances. Over time, simply entering your meditation space can signal to your mind that it is time to relax and focus, making it easier to slip into a meditative state.

Consistency is key when it comes to meditation. Choosing a specific time and place for your practice helps to build a habit that becomes a natural part of your daily routine. Over time, you will find that this dedicated time and space become a sanctuary where you can retreat from the stresses of daily life and find inner peace. Even if your schedule varies, maintaining a sense of regularity— even if it means meditating at different times on different days— helps to reinforce your practice and ensure it remains a priority.

In conclusion, finding the right moment and place to meditate is essential for a successful and enjoyable meditation practice. It should be a time and space that you look forward to, where you can relax and focus on your inner self. By creating a dedicated meditation space and choosing a time that fits your lifestyle, you can enhance your practice and reap the many benefits that meditation offers. As you refine your routine, you will begin to notice the deeper sense of peace, clarity, and mindfulness that arises from a well-established meditation habit.

Emily sat quietly at the edge of the garden patio, sipping her tea, eyes tracing the warm hues of dawn across the sky. Birds softly chirped from nearby trees, adding a gentle soundtrack to the early morning calm. Her day usually began with a rush—checking emails, answering calls, and juggling the chaos of life—but recently, Emily had chosen to create a new morning ritual. This quiet, intentional moment became her sanctuary, a brief pause before the world claimed her attention.

It hadn't always been easy. Finding a time and place to meditate initially felt like yet another task, squeezed into an already overwhelming schedule. But gradually, Emily discovered it was precisely this intentional carving of space that made her days manageable, even enjoyable.

She glanced over at a small corner of the patio, tucked beneath a climbing jasmine vine that released a subtle fragrance into the crisp air. Here she'd placed a small cushion and hung delicate wind chimes. The gentle sounds they made whenever the breeze stirred had become her signal—a call to mindfulness.

The sun climbed higher, warming her skin and signaling the end of her morning meditation. Emily rose feeling grounded and refreshed, her mind clear and ready. Entering the kitchen, she found her husband, David, brewing coffee, his own routine steadfastly different.

"How was meditation today?" David asked gently, pouring himself a cup.

Emily smiled warmly. "Quiet. Just what I needed. You should join me sometime."

David chuckled softly, shaking his head. "Maybe someday. I just can't seem to find the time."

"You don't find time," Emily said playfully. "You make it."

At work, her colleague, Mia, often shared stories of her busy life and how stress seemed to consume her. Today, during their lunch break, Mia sighed deeply, setting her fork down. "Emily, how do you always seem so calm? Honestly, what's your secret?"

Emily paused thoughtfully, choosing her words carefully. "I make space for quiet in my day. It's nothing complicated—just choosing a time and place to slow down. It helps more than you might think."

Mia leaned forward, intrigued. "But when? Where? I barely have enough time to breathe, let alone sit still."

Emily smiled gently. "I felt exactly the same. Start small—just a few minutes somewhere peaceful, even if it's just before bed or early in the morning. Over time, your mind learns to anticipate and cherish that peace. It becomes a refuge."

That evening, Emily returned home to find David in the patio chair, gazing thoughtfully at her meditation corner.

"Something on your mind?" she asked softly, approaching with curiosity.

He shrugged lightly. "Maybe you're right. I've been feeling overwhelmed lately. Could this help me?"

Emily gently placed her hand on his shoulder. "There's only one way to find out."

Together, they decided on a simple evening meditation routine, choosing a quiet indoor space—a small spare room rarely used. Emily carefully cleared clutter, creating an environment that felt calm, inviting, and peaceful. She set up soft lighting, comfortable cushions, and subtle decorations: a few candles, a potted plant, and a favorite inspirational quote framed on the wall.

Their first evening meditation was short, just ten minutes. David shifted uneasily at first but eventually settled into quiet breathing. Afterward, Emily saw him visibly relax, a soft smile emerging on his face.

"That was... surprisingly nice," David admitted quietly.

Days passed into weeks, and soon their evening meditation had become an essential part of their day. It provided clarity, balance, and a shared moment of peace. Emily found herself looking forward to it eagerly—this gentle, quiet time had become a cornerstone of their life.

Months later, Emily and David invited friends over. Mia was among them, sharing how meditation had started transforming her own mornings after Emily's suggestion.

"It feels like breathing again," Mia confessed gratefully. "I found my spot near the window. Watching the sunrise helps me center myself before the chaos begins."

Emily listened with heartfelt joy, recognizing the subtle but powerful ripple effects of choosing the right time and setting for meditation. Each person had their own rhythm, their own special place, and their own unique time of day, but the results were always beautifully similar—clarity, peace, and connection.

That evening, after their friends had left, Emily and David sat together in their meditation room, quietly savoring the tranquility they'd nurtured.

"It feels so natural now, doesn't it?" David mused softly.

"Yes," Emily agreed warmly. "It became easy when we understood it wasn't a chore—it was our sanctuary."

Together they closed their eyes, breathed deeply, and settled comfortably into their meditation, embraced by the quiet serenity of the moment they had consciously chosen.

POSTURE

Stretching

Before we start our actual meditation session, it is always a good idea to stretch and do some light exercises. This will help relax our body when we start meditating, allowing for a smoother transition into a deep meditative state. Stretching helps to release physical tension, improve circulation, and create a sense of ease that supports a prolonged and focused practice. While there is no definitive guide to what stretches and exercises are best, here are a few examples that can be incorporated into your pre-meditation routine:

Neck Rolls – Gently roll your head in a circular motion, first clockwise and then counterclockwise. This helps release tension in the neck and shoulders, areas that often carry stress and tightness. Move slowly and with awareness, noticing any sensations as you stretch.

Shoulder Rolls – Roll your shoulders forward and backward in a circular motion. This loosens up the shoulder muscles and improves posture, preventing discomfort during meditation. Try to synchronize the movement with your breath, inhaling as you lift the shoulders and exhaling as you release them.

Arm Stretches – Extend your arms out to the sides and make small circular movements with your wrists. This helps to relax the arms and wrists, which may otherwise become stiff during long meditation sessions. You can also stretch one arm across your chest and gently press it with your opposite hand to deepen the stretch.

Cat-Cow Stretch – On all fours, arch your back like a cat as you exhale, and then reverse the movement by dropping your belly toward the mat as you inhale. This stretch helps to align the spine, improve flexibility, and release tension in the back, making it easier to sit upright during meditation.

Spinal Twist – Sit cross-legged and gently twist your torso to one side, using your opposite hand to support the twist. Hold the position for a few breaths before switching to the other side. This stretch helps to release tension in the spine and lower back, promoting a more comfortable seated posture.

Hip Circles – Stand with feet hip-width apart and make circular movements with your hips, first clockwise and then counterclockwise. This helps to loosen up the hip joints, which is particularly beneficial if you plan to sit cross-legged for an extended period.

Forward Bend – Stand with feet hip-width apart and bend forward, reaching for your toes. If you cannot reach your toes, simply let your arms hang loosely. This stretch helps to release tension in the hamstrings and lower back, improving flexibility and comfort.

Cobra Pose – Lie on your stomach, place your hands under your shoulders, and gently lift your chest while keeping your shoulders down and back. This pose helps to open the chest, counteracting the tendency to hunch forward, and promotes deep breathing.

Child's Pose – Kneel on the floor, sit back on your heels, and extend your arms in front of you. This pose helps to release tension in the back and shoulders while grounding your energy before meditation. Take slow, deep breaths as you relax into the position.

Ankle Rolls – Sit on the floor and extend one leg out in front of you. Make circular movements with your ankle, first clockwise and then counterclockwise. Repeat with the other leg. This helps to relax the ankles and feet, reducing discomfort during seated meditation.

Wrist Stretches – Extend your arms out in front of you and gently pull your fingers back toward your wrist with the opposite hand. This helps to release tension in the wrists and hands, which can be beneficial if you often hold mudras or gestures during meditation.

Deep Breathing – Sit comfortably and take slow, deep breaths, inhaling through your nose and exhaling through your mouth. This helps to calm the mind and prepare the body for meditation. Deep breathing will be covered in more detail later in this book, but incorporating it into your pre-meditation routine can enhance relaxation.

Incorporating these stretches and exercises into your practice can significantly enhance your meditation experience. They help to relax the body, release tension, and prepare the mind for a deeper and more focused session. Choose the ones that resonate with you and make them a regular part of your practice. Over time, you may find that certain stretches become essential rituals that signal your body and mind to enter a meditative state with greater ease.

Jacob closed his eyes, standing barefoot on the cool wooden floor of his small meditation room. The gentle morning sun filtered through sheer curtains, casting soft golden patterns on the pale walls. It had become Jacob's cherished space, his haven from life's daily pressures.

Before he ever sat to meditate, Jacob had discovered the necessity of first preparing his body. Early attempts at meditation had taught him painfully that sitting still was not enough; tension, restlessness, and discomfort often overwhelmed him, sabotaging the serenity he sought. Thus, he had carefully created a simple but profoundly meaningful prelude to his daily practice: a sequence of stretches.

He began gently, head dipping forward, allowing the weight of gravity to softly pull his chin to his chest. Slowly, with deliberate care, Jacob rolled his head clockwise, savoring each sensation. A slight tightness in his neck began to release, each rotation smoothing out knots of stress lingering from restless sleep. Reversing direction, he felt a quiet gratitude for this simple act of self-care.

Moving naturally into shoulder rolls, Jacob synchronized his movements with his breathing. Shoulders rose gently with his inhale, and softly lowered as he exhaled. Each roll seemed to peel away another thin layer of tension from his upper back. He recalled how often he'd neglected such simple care, carrying his burdens physically in the tightness of his muscles.

Stretching his arms wide, he made gentle circles with his wrists, noticing sensations in his fingers and forearms. It was astonishing how tension accumulated, even there. Jacob then drew one arm across his chest, breathing deeply into the stretch, consciously releasing tension with each breath. He mirrored this with the opposite arm, his body gradually surrendering its lingering stiffness.

Jacob transitioned fluidly to the floor, his palms pressing softly into the smooth surface as he adopted the familiar Cat-Cow posture. With each inhale, his back arched gently downward; with each exhale, it arched upward like a stretching cat. These rhythmic movements brought warmth and flexibility into his spine, freeing stiffness he'd unknowingly carried for days.

After several breaths, he settled into a seated position, crossing his legs comfortably. Here he performed the gentle Spinal Twist, turning slowly to the left, using his breath as an anchor. Then, shifting to the right, each twist softly unlocked deeper layers of tension, bringing soothing relief and quiet anticipation for meditation.

Standing again, Jacob moved into gentle hip circles, smiling inwardly at the simple joy of movement. His hips relaxed, their stiffness melting into warmth, preparing for the comfort of seated stillness.

Then came the Forward Bend, Jacob's favorite. He folded slowly, reaching toward his toes. Though initially his fingertips barely grazed his ankles, with each passing day, he noticed his body responding with greater flexibility and ease. He marveled at the quiet progress he'd made, a testament to the gentle power of consistency and patience.

Lowering himself onto his stomach, Jacob flowed into the Cobra pose, feeling his chest and heart opening gently with each breath. It counteracted hours spent hunched over computers and books, reminding him of the natural openness his body sought.

Moving fluidly from Cobra into Child's Pose, Jacob relaxed completely, forehead touching the ground, arms outstretched comfortably. In this surrendering posture, he felt a profound sense of grounding, his breath deepening, his mind naturally calming.

Before settling fully into meditation, Jacob gently stretched his ankles and wrists, movements small yet purposeful, acknowledging every detail of his physical experience.

Finally, Jacob sat comfortably upright, eyes closed softly, hands resting gently on his knees. With deep, intentional breaths—in through his nose, out through his mouth—he felt the culmination of his careful preparation. The tension he had carried that morning was gone, replaced with ease, openness, and clarity.

In that stillness, Jacob experienced meditation with a depth he'd long sought. The careful, compassionate stretching ritual had become more than mere preparation; it was an act of respect toward himself, an acknowledgment of the inseparable connection between his body and mind.

Later, reflecting on the transformative effect of these simple stretches, Jacob realized their true value: not just physical relaxation, but a powerful symbolic gesture. Each morning's mindful stretching reminded him that meditation was not just something he did—it was a holistic practice, encompassing body, mind, and spirit. And with each mindful stretch, he had learned to enter his meditation naturally, like stepping through an open door into profound peace.

Sitting

The way we sit while meditating is a key component of our sessions, as it directly influences the quality and effectiveness of our practice. While meditation offers numerous benefits, such as reduced stress, improved focus, and enhanced emotional well-being, using poor posture can indeed be detrimental and significantly diminish the benefits we obtain. For this reason, it is crucial to meditate using a good posture.

A good meditation posture is not just about looking straight and tall; it's about creating a balance between alertness and relaxation. Generally speaking, a good posture includes a straight back and a relaxed body. Our spine, upper back, and head must feel aligned and upright, but this alignment should come naturally and not require conscious effort to maintain. Imagine a string attached to the crown of your head, gently pulling you upward, which can help achieve this natural alignment without strain.

To achieve this posture, you can sit on a chair, on the floor with your legs crossed, or even kneel using a meditation bench or cushion. The key is to find a position that allows your hips to be higher than your knees, promoting a natural curve in your lower back. If you're sitting on a chair, ensure your feet are flat on the floor and your thighs are parallel to the ground. If you're sitting on the floor, use a cushion or folded blanket to elevate your hips if needed.

Additionally, the rest of your body—including your arms, legs, and belly—must be relaxed and in a position of no effort. Your arms should rest comfortably on your thighs or in your lap, with your shoulders relaxed and dropped away from your ears. Your legs should be in a position that feels stable and comfortable, whether crossed, straight out in front of you, or bent at the knees with the soles of your feet together. Your belly should be soft and relaxed, allowing for natural breathing.

It's also important to keep your chin slightly tucked in, which helps to align your head with your spine and prevents strain in your neck. Your jaw should be relaxed, and your tongue should rest gently against the roof of your mouth. Your eyes can be closed or softly focused on a point in front of you, whichever feels more comfortable (this concept will be discussed in the next section).

Maintaining a good posture during meditation not only enhances the benefits of your practice but also helps to prevent physical discomfort or injury. It's essential to listen to your body and make adjustments as needed, ensuring that your posture supports your meditation practice rather than hindering it. With consistent practice, maintaining a good posture will become second nature, allowing you to fully immerse yourself in the present moment and reap the full benefits of meditation.

Sophia adjusted her meditation cushion gently, shifting it slightly until it felt just right beneath her hips. Morning sunlight trickled softly through the sheer curtains of her meditation space, illuminating the room with a warm glow. She'd learned from experience how significantly posture affected her sessions, transforming her meditation practice from merely beneficial to truly profound.

When Sophia had first begun meditating, she often sat slouched on her bed or hunched uncomfortably on a chair. Her sessions rarely lasted more than a few distracted minutes before discomfort or restlessness took over. The resulting frustration almost caused her to abandon meditation entirely.

It was during a weekend meditation retreat that she first experienced the transformative power of sitting posture. The instructor, a serene woman named Anya, gently but firmly guided the group in finding proper alignment. Sophia vividly remembered Anya's words: "Imagine a golden thread attached to the crown of your head, gently pulling you upward, straightening your spine without effort."

At first, Sophia felt awkward—holding a position seemed forced, unnatural. Yet, after a few moments of gentle adjustments, something remarkable happened. Her discomfort faded, replaced by a surprising ease. Her breath flowed more naturally, her mind clearer. The rest of the meditation passed in deep tranquility, leaving her feeling centered and energized afterward.

Returning home, Sophia eagerly began applying what she'd learned. Sitting each morning, she consciously visualized that gentle golden thread lifting her upward, aligning her spine effortlessly. Soon, maintaining a proper posture became second nature. Her meditation cushion became an essential ally, raising her hips slightly above her knees, facilitating the natural curve of her lower back.

Sophia discovered the subtle art of balancing alertness and relaxation. She learned how even the smallest adjustments—relaxing her jaw, softening her belly, gently tucking in her chin—dramatically enhanced the quality of her practice. Each part of her posture carried meaning, a quiet conversation with her own body.

One day, her friend Marco, who had begun exploring meditation himself, joined Sophia for a session. Watching him shift uncomfortably, she recognized her past self—tense, distracted, and frustrated.

"Try elevating your hips slightly," Sophia suggested softly, handing Marco a spare cushion. "Your knees should rest comfortably lower than your hips. It feels strange at first, but it helps."

Marco adjusted reluctantly, skepticism evident in his eyes. But within minutes, his breathing slowed, his expression relaxed, and a peaceful calm settled upon him. Afterward, he looked genuinely astonished.

"I can't believe how much difference that made," he admitted with a smile. "It's like my body found peace, and my mind followed."

Sophia nodded warmly. "That's exactly how it felt for me. Our bodies and minds aren't separate—they support each other."

Encouraged by Marco's experience, Sophia began teaching others in her community, emphasizing the simple yet profound importance of proper sitting posture. Whether sitting cross-legged on cushions, kneeling on meditation benches, or seated comfortably in chairs, her students soon discovered for themselves the powerful connection between body alignment and mental clarity.

Months passed, and Sophia's small meditation room became a refuge for friends, neighbors, and even strangers seeking guidance. Through mindful sitting, they collectively experienced deeper relaxation, greater emotional resilience, and improved physical well-being. Many expressed surprise at how something as seemingly insignificant as posture could hold such power.

One evening, as Sophia sat quietly after a long day's work, she reflected deeply on this journey. Her meditation cushion felt comforting beneath her, the posture natural and effortless. It struck her profoundly that this simple act of sitting properly had transformed not just her meditation practice but her life.

Sitting became more than a physical act—it was symbolic. Sophia realized that good posture was, at its heart, about self-respect, self-awareness, and mindful presence. Each moment spent aligning her body, releasing tension, and focusing her attention had subtly but powerfully reshaped her relationship with herself.

In that moment, sitting quietly, she felt an overwhelming gratitude—not just for meditation itself, but for every small detail she'd learned along the way. She now understood posture not simply as a step toward meditation, but as meditation itself—an ongoing practice of awareness, self-care, and profound inner connection.

Sophia took a slow, deep breath, savoring the peaceful clarity of the moment. In the simplicity of sitting upright, relaxed yet alert, she found a quiet joy, knowing she'd discovered a lifelong key to mindfulness and inner peace.

Eyes

Whether you start off by keeping your eyes gently open or fully closed is entirely up to you, as both approaches have their merits. However, most advanced meditation practices truly require your eyes to be closed. This is because closing your eyes helps to minimize distractions from the external environment, allowing you to focus more deeply on your inner experiences.

At the beginning of your meditation journey, opening your eyes and focusing on an object, such as a candle flame, a dot on the wall, or a natural scene, can help achieve some initial progress. This technique, in some meditation traditions, is used to improve concentration and focus. Some experts even use this approach for advanced practices to cultivate a steady gaze and enhance mental clarity. A technique known as fixed-gaze meditation, involves staring at an external object, often a candle flame, without blinking for as long as possible. This practice is believed to strengthen concentration, cleanse the eyes, and prepare the mind for deeper meditation. Nevertheless, in this book, we will be focusing on practices that involve closing your eyes entirely.

It is true that closing your eyes has the initial drawback of potentially inducing sleep, especially if you are new to meditation or if you are meditating in a comfortable or dimly lit environment. However, if you are sitting in a good posture, as discussed earlier, if you were to start to fall asleep, your head would automatically nod, or your body would shift, bringing you back to a state of wakefulness. This natural feedback mechanism helps maintain awareness while still allowing deep relaxation. Additionally, closing your eyes fully immerses you into your inner world, where most of the meditational activity takes place. This inner world is rich with sensations, thoughts, and emotions that can be explored and understood more deeply when your eyes are closed.

For some, keeping the eyes closed might initially lead to increased mental chatter, as there are fewer external stimuli to anchor awareness. If this happens, you may find it helpful to focus on a specific meditation technique, such as mindful breathing, mantra repetition, or body scanning, to gently guide your attention inward. Over time, the tendency of the mind to wander will lessen, and closing the eyes will become a more natural part of the practice.

This being said, it is perfectly okay if you start off the session with your eyes open and perform a few breathing exercises to help you settle into the practice. This can be particularly helpful if you feel anxious or restless at the beginning of your meditation session. Some practitioners find it useful to start with a soft gaze, looking slightly downward with unfocused vision, before gradually closing their eyes. However, as soon as it feels comfortable, you should try to keep your eyes closed. Note that your eyes should be closed, but relaxed at the same time. There should be no tension or strain in your eye muscles. You can gently close your eyes and allow them to rest naturally, without forcing them shut.

As you close your eyes, you may begin the actual meditation session. Take a moment to scan your body and ensure that you are comfortable and relaxed. If you notice any areas of tension, take a few deep breaths and allow that tension to release. You may also become aware of the natural play of light behind your closed eyelids—subtle patterns, colors, or darkness. Instead of focusing on them, simply acknowledge their presence and let your attention return to your chosen meditation focus. Once you feel settled, you can begin to focus on your breath, a mantra, or a specific meditation technique, allowing your awareness to deepen and your mind to quiet.

It's also worth noting that some meditation practices, such as mindfulness of the senses or body scan meditations, may involve opening your eyes at certain points to bring awareness to the external environment. In certain mindfulness traditions, practitioners are encouraged to practice with their eyes half-open, maintaining awareness of both their internal and external surroundings simultaneously. This method is particularly useful for integrating mindfulness into daily life, as it trains the mind to remain present regardless of whether the eyes are open or closed.

However, for the majority of meditation practices, closing your eyes is the most effective way to cultivate inner awareness and focus. With consistent practice, you will become more comfortable with closing your eyes during meditation and will be able to fully immerse yourself in the present moment, reaping the full benefits of your practice. Over time, you will develop the ability to enter a meditative state with greater ease, and the distinction between the external world and the inner world will become less pronounced, allowing for deeper states of awareness and tranquility.

Lena sat comfortably on her meditation cushion, feeling the gentle warmth of early sunlight filtering softly through her window. The peaceful morning atmosphere was broken only by distant birdsong, a natural melody to accompany her quiet contemplation. Lena had come to treasure these early mornings, moments of silence in an otherwise bustling life.

She had begun meditation a few months prior, discovering quickly that her eyes, of all things, posed an unexpected challenge. Initially, keeping her eyes closed during meditation felt unnatural and surprisingly unsettling. The darkness behind closed eyelids had been disorienting, and Lena often found herself drifting into sleep rather than achieving the clarity she sought.

Frustrated, she consulted her friend, Eli, who had practiced meditation for years. Eli patiently listened and nodded knowingly, offering gentle advice. "Try meditating with your eyes softly open at first. Focus on something simple—a candle flame or a flower—anything steady that allows your attention to settle naturally. Gradually, you'll find it easier to close your eyes without drifting into sleep."

Taking Eli's advice, Lena began her next meditation session with a small candle placed carefully before her. The flame flickered softly, mesmerizing in its gentle dance. She gazed steadily at the flame, allowing her breathing to synchronize naturally with the subtle movements of the light.

At first, the external object anchored her restless mind, bringing a soothing calm she hadn't experienced before. Over several days, her gaze became steadier, her concentration deepening naturally. The candle flame seemed not just external, but somehow internal—mirroring her breathing, her heartbeat, and the quieting of her mind.

Eventually, Lena felt ready to attempt closing her eyes again. This time, however, instead of the disorienting darkness she'd previously encountered, she noticed a calm inner space opening within her. The external flame seemed to continue glowing gently behind her closed eyelids, imprinted into her mind's eye as a comforting presence.

Days turned into weeks, and Lena's meditation practice blossomed. She began effortlessly transitioning from softly open eyes to fully closed eyes within a single session. She found herself drawn more profoundly into her internal experience, exploring layers of thought, sensation, and emotion with growing ease.

One morning, Lena invited Eli to meditate with her. They sat quietly facing each other, a candle flickering gently between them. Afterward, Lena shared her experience: "Closing my eyes became easier when I first used an external focus. Now, even when my eyes are closed, I feel as if I can still see, just differently."

Eli smiled warmly, nodding in understanding. "Exactly. Meditation helps us see in a different way—beyond physical sight. It's not about blindness to the world but about opening inner eyes. Eventually, your inner and outer worlds blend into a single experience of mindful awareness."

Lena continued exploring these subtleties. Occasionally, she experimented with fixed-gaze meditation, gently staring at the flame without blinking until tears softened her gaze. This strengthened her concentration further, refining her ability to remain attentive and present. Other times, she practiced mindfulness meditation with eyes half-open, effortlessly balancing inner awareness with gentle recognition of her external environment.

One evening, during a quiet meditation retreat, Lena found herself particularly restless. Her mind wandered uncontrollably, anxiety creeping into her awareness. Remembering Eli's words, she allowed her eyes to gently open, softly resting on the candle before her. Gradually, her anxiety lessened, her breath slowed, and the room's subtle details—the flame's glow, the gentle dance of shadows—brought her back to tranquility.

The experience deepened Lena's understanding of meditation. It was not merely about closing her eyes and escaping inward but about developing flexibility and mastery over her attention. She learned the art of gently guiding her awareness, eyes open or closed, depending on what her mind and heart needed most in the moment.

Returning home after the retreat, Lena found her practice had deepened significantly. Closing her eyes now felt natural, comforting, and no longer disorienting. Behind her eyelids, she sensed a vibrant inner landscape—patterns of soft color, subtle movements of energy—never distracting, always enriching.

Months later, Lena visited Eli again, eager to share her insights. Sitting in Eli's quiet garden, sunlight illuminating the space gently, Lena spoke softly, "It's as if closing my eyes has opened a new world within. But knowing when and how to open them again is equally important. Meditation is balance—being fully present, eyes open or closed."

Eli nodded deeply, smiling with pride. "You've discovered the essence of meditation. It's a practice of internal seeing, flexible and responsive, deeply attuned to the present."

Lena left Eli's garden that day profoundly grateful. She now understood clearly how the seemingly simple choice of opening or closing her eyes during meditation profoundly influenced her inner journey. Meditation had taught her to truly see—not merely through her physical eyes, but through an inner gaze that blended seamlessly with her experience of life itself.

In this newfound clarity, Lena felt a quiet, lasting joy—a realization that her journey inward was just beginning, enriched by each moment spent in mindful awareness, eyes gently closed or softly open, ready to fully embrace whatever each moment brought forth.

BREATHING

Basics

Breathing is arguably the most vital and complex aspect of meditation, requiring dedicated practice and patience to truly master. While other components, such as posture and eye positioning, can become habitual for many practitioners within a few weeks, breathing is a deeply ingrained, automatic function of the body, making it one of the most challenging aspects to retrain. Achieving mastery over breath control is not merely a technical endeavor; it is a gradual transformation that can take months or even years to refine. The subtleties of proper breathing extend beyond conscious effort—they demand awareness, consistency, and an intimate understanding of one's own physiological and mental rhythms.

One of the foundational breathing techniques in meditation, and indeed the bedrock upon which all other techniques are built, is belly breathing, also known as diaphragmatic breathing. This method is central to nearly every meditation tradition, serving as both an entry point for beginners and a powerful tool that even advanced practitioners return to. By mastering belly breathing, we re-establish a connection to our natural breath, creating a stable foundation upon which deeper, more advanced techniques can be explored.

From a theoretical standpoint, diaphragmatic breathing is our body's innate way of breathing—it is the way infants breathe effortlessly, with each inhale and exhale flowing in perfect harmony. However, as we grow older, factors such as stress, poor posture, environmental conditioning, and habitual shallow breathing often lead us to disconnect from this natural rhythm. Many adults unconsciously develop the habit of breathing shallowly from the chest rather than deeply from the diaphragm. Over time, this shift can create unnecessary tension in the body, contribute to anxiety, and reduce overall oxygen efficiency.

Relearning how to breathe deeply from the belly can feel unfamiliar at first, but once this technique is restored and integrated, its benefits become immediately apparent. Many practitioners notice an almost instant improvement in relaxation, mental clarity, and emotional regulation, even without engaging in more advanced meditative practices. In fact, for some, belly breathing alone can bring them into profound states of meditation, allowing them to experience heightened awareness, tranquility, and deep introspection.

At its core, belly breathing is simple: the belly should remain completely relaxed and expand naturally with each inhale, and retract fully with each exhale. However, the key lies in ensuring that this movement is effortless, unforced, and deeply natural. Straining or controlling the breath too aggressively disrupts the meditative flow, leading to tension rather than relaxation.

To properly practice belly breathing, one must first find a comfortable position, whether seated with an upright spine or lying down if that feels more natural. Placing one hand gently on the chest and the other on the belly can serve as a helpful guide, allowing the practitioner to observe how the breath moves through the body. As the inhale is drawn in, the belly should expand outward while the chest remains still, indicating that the diaphragm is engaged. As the exhale flows out, the belly should retract naturally, releasing all the air without force or strain. There may be an initial tendency to over-breathe, inhaling more deeply than necessary or exhaling beyond the body's natural rhythm, but with time and practice, the breath will regulate itself into a smooth, effortless cycle.

Belly breathing is not just about the physical act of inhaling and exhaling; it is also about cultivating an awareness of the breath as a focal point of meditation. By paying close attention to the rhythm, depth, and sensation of each breath, one begins to develop a heightened sense of presence. As distractions, emotions, and wandering thoughts arise, the breath serves as an anchor, gently guiding the mind back to a state of centeredness.

With regular practice, belly breathing will naturally integrate into daily life, extending beyond the meditation cushion into every moment. Many practitioners find that as this technique becomes second nature, their everyday breathing patterns shift, leading to a calmer state of being, greater emotional stability, and enhanced focus. This foundational practice not only improves overall well-being but also prepares the mind and body for more advanced breathwork techniques. Those who wish to explore deeper meditative states, such as energy circulation, breath retention, or the subtle interactions of solar and lunar breathing, must first develop a mastery of this fundamental technique.

Perfecting belly breathing is a long-term practice, one that requires patience and dedication, but its rewards are immense. With every breath, the practitioner cultivates a deeper connection to their body, mind, and awareness itself, making each inhale and exhale not just a physical necessity, but a step toward inner peace and self-discovery.

Lucas sat quietly on the edge of his bed, early morning light filtering softly through his bedroom curtains. For months now, his daily routine had included meditation, yet something always felt slightly incomplete. He had learned about posture, the importance of setting, and the nuances of opening or closing his eyes, but the breathing—something so fundamental, so basic—still eluded him.

At first, Lucas found breathing exercises tedious. Breathing was automatic, something he'd done unconsciously for his entire life. Trying to control or even focus on it felt unnatural and forced. But, determined to deepen his practice, Lucas committed to mastering belly breathing, convinced it held the key to unlocking deeper meditation.

The first day of this new practice was discouraging. Sitting cross-legged, Lucas placed one hand gently on his chest and another on his belly. As instructed, he inhaled deeply, striving to feel his belly expand. Instead, he noticed his chest rising and falling rapidly, his breath shallow and uneasy.

"Why is something so basic so difficult?" Lucas murmured, frustration simmering beneath the surface.

He shared his struggles with his meditation teacher, Anna, during their next meeting. Anna listened patiently, smiling softly, understanding clear in her eyes.

"Breathing is simple," she acknowledged gently. "But our habits complicate it. You're not just retraining your breath; you're reconnecting with your body's natural wisdom."

Lucas decided to approach his practice with renewed patience. The next morning, instead of rushing, he allowed himself to simply sit and observe his natural breath. Gradually, gently, he guided his awareness toward his belly, quietly inviting deeper breaths without force or frustration.

Over days, he discovered subtle improvements. His belly began responding naturally, expanding effortlessly with inhales and *relaxing smoothly with exhales. His chest remained calmer, his breath less hurried. Lucas started feeling an unexpected calmness, something deeply peaceful and grounding.*

The transformation wasn't limited to his meditation cushion. One afternoon at work, confronted by a sudden, stressful deadline, Lucas instinctively placed his hand softly on his belly. Almost immediately, his breath slowed, deepening naturally. His anxiety softened, clarity returned, and the deadline became manageable.

Inspired by these small victories, Lucas explored deeper into belly breathing. Anna encouraged him to visualize his breath as gentle waves rising and falling within him, effortlessly matching his natural rhythm. Each day, Lucas felt a stronger connection to this imagery, sensing his inner rhythms aligning harmoniously with each breath.

Weeks passed into months. Lucas's practice deepened profoundly. His meditations lengthened effortlessly, driven by his rhythmic breathing. Each inhale and exhale felt smooth, unforced, and soothing. During meditation, distractions arose less frequently, and when they did, Lucas found it easier than ever to gently redirect his awareness back to his breath.

One day, Lucas joined a meditation workshop Anna was leading in a serene retreat center, surrounded by quiet woods and softly chirping birds. Seated comfortably among others, Lucas listened as Anna guided the group through belly breathing.

"Place one hand gently on your belly," Anna instructed calmly, her voice soft and reassuring. "Allow your breath to deepen naturally. Notice how your belly expands effortlessly as you inhale and gently releases as you exhale."

As Lucas followed her guidance, he marveled at how effortlessly his breath flowed now, compared to those frustrating first days. He noticed the calm spreading throughout his body, a profound peace settling within him. Opening his eyes afterward, he saw the relaxed faces of those around him, many clearly experiencing deep tranquility for the first time.

After the workshop, several participants approached Lucas, asking questions about their struggles with breathing, their experiences mirroring his own initial difficulties. Smiling warmly, Lucas offered gentle reassurance, sharing his own journey.

"It takes patience," he said softly, recalling Anna's wisdom. "But breathing deeply becomes natural once we learn to trust our body's innate rhythm."

Returning home, Lucas felt inspired to help others discover this foundational skill. He began leading small meditation groups, emphasizing belly breathing's simplicity and power. His students, initially skeptical, soon found their anxieties easing, their sleep improving, and their emotional resilience strengthening.

As Lucas continued his teaching, he discovered another subtle truth—breathing was not merely a technique but a lifelong practice, deeply intertwined with every aspect of living. He began noticing how breathing influenced every moment—conversations became calmer, stressful situations more manageable, and even joyful moments richer.

One evening, sitting quietly in his meditation space, Lucas reflected deeply on his journey. Belly breathing had transformed his meditation from frustrating to fulfilling, his life from chaotic to balanced. Each breath felt like a gentle affirmation, reminding him of the calm he now carried within.

As he closed his eyes that evening, Lucas felt immense gratitude. The simple act of breathing deeply, something once so difficult and foreign, had become his greatest source of inner peace. In every breath, Lucas now felt the presence of tranquility, clarity, and a profound connection to himself.

Breathing deeply, Lucas smiled gently, fully aware that while his journey had begun with something as basic as breath, it had evolved into an endless, beautiful exploration—an ongoing conversation between himself and the profound wisdom of his own breath.

Nose Breath

So far, we have explored the foundational aspects of breathing, beginning with the basic principles of breath awareness and the essential technique of belly breathing. Now, we turn to a more refined and esoteric practice: nose breathing. As with all deeper meditative techniques, true understanding does not come solely from reading about them but from direct experience and persistent practice. The subtleties involved in such methods often require years of refinement, personal experimentation, and, in some cases, direct guidance from seasoned practitioners. Those who seek a fuller understanding may find great benefit in engaging with fellow meditators, attending workshops, or seeking specialized instruction, as some nuances can only be fully grasped through shared experience and real-time feedback.

Despite the complexities of these practices, the most important elements remain perseverance and consistency. Time itself becomes the teacher, gradually revealing the deeper layers of understanding that cannot be accessed through intellectual pursuit alone. Even without external guidance, the dedicated practitioner will, through patient effort, begin to uncover insights that were previously obscured. Meditation, after all, is a process of unveiling, of peeling back the layers of perception to reveal an ever-deepening awareness of the self. It is within this spirit that we now turn to the technique of nose breathing.

Also known as lunar breathing, nose breathing consists of inhaling and exhaling exclusively through the nose while maintaining the principles of belly breathing. The breath must flow smoothly, without interruption or force, maintaining an even, natural rhythm. As we cultivate this method, we begin to notice an underlying current within the breath itself—a subtle, almost imperceptible energy that fills the body. This energy, often described as "white" in nature, moves fluidly, shifting and adapting according to our emotional state and level of practice. While this aspect of the breath will reveal its intricacies over time, the primary goal at this stage is simply to observe.

By paying close attention to the breath as it enters and exits through the nose, we gradually develop the ability to perceive its movement in greater detail. For many, the breath appears to take on a tangible shape, a flowing path within the body that changes in response to our awareness. In its most common form, the breath seems to travel from the nose down to the belly on the inhale, and from the belly back up to the nose on the exhale. However, with deeper practice, these patterns will begin to shift, tracing new and unexpected paths through the body. Rather than attempting to impose control or direct these movements, the key is to remain in a state of pure observation, allowing the breath to follow its natural course.

As sensitivity increases, it is also common to notice an intricate relationship between breath and heartbeat. At times, each inhalation and exhalation may seem to create a rhythmic pulse in various parts of the body—most notably in the heart, belly, or even the head. This phenomenon is a natural sign of progress, an indication that breath and awareness are beginning to synchronize on a deeper level. Once again, the approach remains the same: observe without interference, letting these sensations unfold without resistance.

As these experiences become more frequent, they signal readiness for the next stage of practice: throat breathing. This advanced technique builds directly upon the foundations established through nose breathing, adding new dimensions of awareness and control to the meditative process. However, before moving forward, it is essential to attain mastery of nose breathing. Without a firm grasp of this technique, the intricacies of throat breathing will remain elusive, and its full benefits will not be realized. The path of breath mastery unfolds in stages, each building upon the last, and only through patience and diligent practice can one progress naturally and effectively.

Oliver sat quietly in the gentle shadows of his meditation room, early morning sunlight just beginning to brush softly against the drawn curtains. His breathing was steady, calm, flowing effortlessly through his nostrils. Each breath felt smooth, natural, and utterly serene. He had spent months mastering basic breath awareness and belly breathing, and now he felt ready to delve deeper into the subtle practice known as nose breathing.

He first learned of this technique at a weekend meditation retreat, guided by Elena, a gentle teacher whose quiet strength and calm presence had resonated deeply with Oliver. She spoke briefly but meaningfully about nose breathing, emphasizing that true understanding came only through experience, patience, and consistent effort. Intrigued, Oliver had dedicated himself to this practice wholeheartedly upon returning home.

The initial weeks were challenging. Oliver found it surprisingly difficult to maintain exclusive nasal breathing without slipping into old habits. His breath felt restricted, occasionally forced. Frustration surfaced regularly, tempting him to return to the comfort of familiar methods. Yet Elena's words echoed persistently in his mind: patience, persistence, observation without interference.

With gentle determination, Oliver continued. Each morning, sitting cross-legged on his cushion, he breathed slowly, intentionally, through his nose. Gradually, the initial resistance softened into ease. He began noticing subtle shifts within each breath—a quiet energy, delicate and barely perceptible at first, gently flowing downward from his nostrils, expanding into his belly, and rising softly back upward again.

Over weeks, the sensations intensified, evolving into something he could almost visualize—a smooth, white current that moved harmoniously within him. Oliver marveled at this inner rhythm, fascinated by its adaptability, changing subtly according to his emotional state. When calm, the energy felt gentle and expansive;

when restless or stressed, the energy became denser, more focused.

One afternoon, while sharing tea after class, Oliver confided in Elena about these subtle experiences. She listened attentively, nodding with quiet understanding.

"What you're describing is the natural progression," Elena explained softly. "As you deepen your awareness, your breath reveals more of itself. Stay observant, remain patient, and let it unfold naturally."

Oliver took her words to heart, returning home more motivated than ever. Each session became an exploration, an invitation to witness and understand his own inner workings. With every breath, Oliver felt more attuned to the subtle interplay between physical sensations, emotional states, and inner energy.

As his sensitivity deepened, Oliver began noticing intricate connections between his breath and heartbeat. Occasionally, each inhalation seemed to echo rhythmically within his chest, subtly influencing the pace of his heart. The phenomenon was subtle yet profound—a rhythmic dance between breath and pulse, drawing him deeper into meditation.

Months into the practice, Oliver experienced a particularly vivid meditation. Sitting calmly, breathing quietly through his nose, he felt suddenly aware of a delicate pulse synchronizing with his breath—not just in his heart, but spreading throughout his body. Each breath seemed to ripple gently through his limbs, fingertips, and even his head. It was as if his breath had become a gentle tide, washing softly over every cell.

Astonished by this newfound depth, Oliver sought out Elena again, eager to understand this remarkable experience. She smiled knowingly as he described it, recognizing his progress.

"You're discovering the deeper layers of nose breathing," Elena explained patiently. "When your breath and awareness align, they

naturally synchronize with your heartbeat and other rhythms in your body. It signals you're ready for the next stage—throat breathing—but first, master this. Allow yourself to fully integrate these insights."

Oliver accepted her guidance humbly, aware that rushing forward would hinder rather than enhance his practice. Returning home, he continued refining nose breathing, each session revealing new subtleties. His meditations became longer, richer, more deeply satisfying. The distinction between his internal world and external reality blurred subtly, creating a seamless sense of presence.

The calm cultivated through nose breathing seeped quietly into his daily life, influencing every interaction, every decision. Oliver found himself more patient, more compassionate, and profoundly aware of the interconnectedness of breath, mind, and emotion.

One evening, sitting in quiet meditation, Oliver felt an overwhelming sense of gratitude for this gentle yet powerful practice. Nose breathing had not just deepened his meditation; it had transformed him subtly but unmistakably. Breathing quietly, he smiled, fully aware that the journey was far from over.

In each breath, Oliver now sensed not only tranquility but infinite possibility—the continual unfolding of awareness, the delicate balance of observation and experience. He understood clearly now that mastery of breath was not merely technical—it was a lifelong, profound conversation with himself.

As he breathed gently through his nose, fully immersed in that quiet moment, Oliver realized that nose breathing had become more than a meditation technique—it had become the language of his inner peace, the gentle rhythm guiding him ever deeper into understanding himself and the profound stillness within.

Throat Breath

Throat breathing, often referred to as solar breathing, is an advanced and deeply esoteric technique. Unlike lunar breathing, which is relatively straightforward in its execution even if its effects remain subtle, solar breathing requires a level of understanding and control that is both more intricate and more challenging to master. The difficulty lies not only in its mechanics but also in the ability to attune oneself to the energy shifts it creates within the body. While lunar breathing primarily involves passive observation, solar breathing introduces an element of intentional modulation that must be performed with both precision and awareness.

A helpful way to conceptualize this technique is to compare it to whispering. In daily life, when we whisper, we engage the throat to regulate airflow, creating a soft, hushed sound. The same principle applies when one is startled and instinctively gasps, producing a whisper-like sound while inhaling. This is key to understanding solar breathing: just as it is possible to whisper while both exhaling and inhaling, solar breathing employs this same dynamic. Imagine yourself in a situation where you must whisper a secret with utmost caution, ensuring that no one else can hear. Now, take this whispering breath and apply it not only to your exhalation but also to your inhalation, maintaining a continuous, controlled airflow.

Esoteric concepts are often conveyed through metaphors, imagery, and ritual, as they are difficult to describe in purely logical terms. Many traditions use symbols and elaborate explanations to communicate the nuances of these practices. However, thinking of solar breathing as a controlled whisper—a breath that maintains a hushed, flowing sound in both directions—provides an accessible and tangible way to grasp the technique. This method removes unnecessary complexity and allows for a more intuitive understanding of how the breath interacts with the throat.

Once this concept is clear, the next step is to produce the breath's signature whispering sound without actually forming words. Instead of shaping syllables, allow the air to pass freely, generating a soft, steady sound, much like the wind rustling through leaves. This should be done while maintaining full diaphragmatic breathing, ensuring that the breath remains deep, steady, and effortless. Straining or forcing the breath will be counterproductive, creating unnecessary tension that disrupts the natural flow. The breath should feel as though it is moving through the throat like a gentle current, guided by subtle control rather than conscious effort.

As the technique deepens, an important distinction emerges between lunar and solar breathing. Whereas lunar breathing produces a white energy that moves through the body in flowing paths, solar breathing generates an entirely different sensation—one that feels more centralized and intense. The energy produced by solar breathing is not white but red, and instead of tracing paths or synchronizing with the heartbeat, it forms a central point that radiates outward in waves. This pattern is much like the ripples created when a stone is dropped into still water—originating from a single focal point and expanding outward in concentric circles. This visualization can be a useful guide, offering insight into the nature of the energetic shifts taking place.

As with lunar breathing, the primary goal is observation rather than control. It is crucial to resist the urge to manipulate or force these energy movements; instead, simply allow the breath to flow naturally and take note of the changes it creates within the body. The contrast between lunar and solar breathing will become increasingly apparent with practice, revealing the unique characteristics and benefits of each technique.

Solar breathing can be intense, making it less suitable for beginners. It is essential to establish a firm foundation in diaphragmatic breathing and lunar breathing before attempting this more advanced practice. Without this groundwork, the subtleties of solar breathing may be difficult to perceive, and its effects may feel overwhelming. As with all esoteric techniques, patience and gentleness are key. Progress unfolds gradually, and with time, solar breathing will become a powerful tool for deepening one's meditation practice, offering profound insights into the interplay between breath, energy, and awareness.

Clara sat quietly in the warm glow of candlelight, her meditation room infused with a gentle sense of serenity. Her breathing was calm, rhythmic, and deep, a gentle whisper moving effortlessly through her throat. Months of disciplined practice had led her here, to this subtle yet powerful technique known as throat breathing, or solar breathing.

She vividly remembered her initial encounter with solar breathing during a workshop taught by her mentor, Isabel. Unlike earlier practices, solar breathing demanded a greater precision, patience, and sensitivity. Isabel had explained it carefully, comparing the breath to a controlled whisper, reminding the class of moments when one whispers carefully, urgently, the sound hushed but intentional.

In the beginning, Clara struggled. Her first attempts felt unnatural, forced, and frustratingly difficult to maintain. Her throat tightened with strain, her breath uneven and uncomfortable. Many evenings, she sat in silent frustration, questioning whether she was ready for this advanced technique. Yet Isabel's gentle encouragement kept her determined.

"Think of your breath as whispering," Isabel had reassured her quietly after class one evening. "You're whispering inwardly, softly guiding the breath both in and out, like a quiet secret you must guard carefully. It must flow naturally, effortlessly."

Clara took this advice to heart, returning home determined but gentle with herself. Sitting calmly, she began by whispering softly, feeling the breath flow through her throat, and gradually shifted to the whisper-like breathing Isabel described. With practice, the forced tension lessened, replaced by a newfound ease.

After weeks of gentle effort, Clara began to notice subtle shifts. The breathing transformed from an awkward effort into a smooth, flowing current. Her throat no longer strained; instead, it guided the breath effortlessly, maintaining a gentle whispering sound that flowed continuously inward and outward.

As this practice deepened, Clara noticed something remarkable —each breath created subtle shifts in energy within her body. While lunar breathing had given her an expansive, flowing sensation, this was different. Solar breathing produced a focused, intense energy that radiated outward from a central point deep within her chest, pulsating gently like ripples expanding on water.

Intrigued by this new sensation, Clara sought Isabel's wisdom once more.

"You're perceiving the subtle energy of solar breathing," Isabel confirmed gently, smiling warmly. "Unlike lunar breathing, this energy is more intense and focused. It originates from within and moves outward. Observe this sensation without trying to control it, letting the breath guide your awareness."

Taking Isabel's words to heart, Clara continued her practice, deepening her awareness each day. With patience and curiosity, she observed how each breath created concentric waves of gentle yet powerful energy. At times, it felt overwhelming, almost too intense, but Clara reminded herself always to observe without interference.

Gradually, Clara's perception of this red, solar energy intensified. Each session revealed deeper layers of subtlety, the energy radiating outward more vividly, her entire body responding harmoniously. It felt as though her breath had become a living force, whispering a profound inner secret that resonated throughout her being.

Her practice soon attracted the attention of her close friend, Mia, who was intrigued by Clara's newfound sense of calm and clarity.

"How is this solar breathing different?" Mia asked curiously during a quiet afternoon together.

"It feels like whispering," Clara explained softly, recalling Isabel's metaphor. "Instead of breathing openly, you gently guide the breath through your throat, creating this quiet, whispering flow. The energy feels more focused, intense, radiating outward rather than flowing through you."

Mia listened carefully, fascinated by the subtle complexities of this advanced technique. Encouraged by Clara, she began exploring solar breathing herself, quickly discovering its challenges but also glimpsing its potential.

Weeks later, during a weekend retreat, Isabel invited Clara to guide a small group through solar breathing. Nervous but honored, Clara accepted, carefully explaining the whispering technique, the soft sound produced by the controlled passage of air through the throat, and the gentle observation of energy radiating outward.

As she guided the session, Clara felt a profound sense of connection—not just with her own practice but with those around her. Together, they shared the subtle yet powerful experience of solar breathing, feeling its focused energy harmonizing among them.

Afterward, participants approached Clara gratefully, sharing their experiences of clarity, warmth, and newfound awareness. Clara felt humbled and deeply joyful, realizing she had not just deepened her own practice but had become a channel to share this profound technique.

Returning home from the retreat, Clara continued refining her practice. Throat breathing had transformed her meditation profoundly, creating a deeper connection to herself and an enhanced sensitivity to the subtle movements of energy within her.

One evening, sitting alone in her meditation space, Clara reflected deeply on her journey. What had once felt difficult and unnatural now flowed effortlessly, each whispering breath connecting her profoundly to her inner essence. She felt immense gratitude for the challenges that had guided her here and the profound insights gained along the way.

As she breathed gently, whispering softly inward and outward, Clara understood clearly that throat breathing was not just a technique—it had become an intimate dialogue with herself. Each whispering breath revealed new depths of inner peace, profound connection, and subtle power.

In that quiet moment, fully immersed in her practice, Clara smiled gently, aware that the journey of solar breathing was endless—each breath an invitation to delve ever deeper into the mysteries of self-awareness, presence, and profound inner tranquility.

Storm Breathing

Although there are many ways to combine lunar and solar breathing, the fundamental method involves inhaling through lunar breathing (nose breathing) and exhaling through solar breathing (throat breathing). This combination creates a dynamic and powerful meditative experience, integrating the distinct energies associated with each technique.

The sensation of this practice can be compared to a bolt of lightning striking as you inhale and the deep, rolling sound of thunder as you exhale. Because of this, some traditions refer to it as Storm Breathing. The imagery of a storm effectively captures the nature of this practice—where inhalation brings a sudden, powerful surge of energy, and exhalation releases it in a prolonged and resonant manner.

The direction or shape that this energetic "lightning" takes is not always fixed. It may not always feel as if it is striking the ground. Sometimes, the breath might seem to move toward the left or right side of the body. Other times, it may feel like it bolts into the sky, behind your back, or spreads outward in unexpected ways. These variations are influenced by factors such as emotional state, posture, and the specific intentions you bring to your meditation practice.

Rather than trying to control these movements, it is essential to approach this technique with openness and observation. The goal is not to dictate the breath's direction or force a particular sensation but to notice the subtle shifts that occur naturally. Let go of any need to manipulate the experience and simply observe how the energy moves, what shapes it takes, and what feelings arise. Through this process, a deeper understanding of the subtle energetic flows within the body will emerge.

To practice Storm Breathing, begin in a comfortable seated position with a straight back and a relaxed body. Take a few deep diaphragmatic breaths to center yourself. As you inhale, draw the breath deeply into your lungs through your nose, allowing your belly to expand fully. As you exhale, engage the throat to modulate the airflow, producing a soft whispering sound, much like the resonance of distant thunder. Allow the breath to flow effortlessly, observing the energy's path and shape without interference.

With time and consistent practice, you will become more attuned to the unique qualities of Storm Breathing and the distinct energetic effects it produces. This technique can lead to profound meditative states, enhancing awareness, focus, and overall well-being. As with all advanced meditation practices, it is essential to approach Storm Breathing with patience, gentleness, and a willingness to explore the subtle energies within yourself.

Daniel settled onto his meditation cushion, the sky outside heavy with dark clouds, the distant rumble of an approaching storm vibrating softly through his quiet apartment. A deep sense of anticipation filled the air—perfectly fitting, Daniel thought, for the practice he was about to begin. Today, he intended to explore Storm Breathing, an advanced technique he had learned from his meditation teacher, Adrian.

Storm Breathing intrigued Daniel from the moment Adrian described it. Combining the subtle lunar breathing—calm inhalations through the nose—with the intense solar breathing— whisper-like exhalations through the throat—promised a meditative experience unlike anything he had encountered. Adrian had poetically compared the practice to a storm: a sudden, electrifying inhale like lightning, followed by a deep, rolling exhale like thunder.

As Daniel settled deeper, he began by taking several grounding breaths, inhaling gently through his nose and exhaling quietly through his mouth. Gradually, he shifted into lunar breathing, inhaling smoothly through his nose, feeling a gentle energy flow into his belly. With each exhale, he transitioned into solar breathing, a whisper resonating softly through his throat.

At first, the combination felt awkward, his throat tense, his breathing uneven. But Daniel reminded himself of Adrian's gentle guidance: "Observe without forcing. Let your breath become the storm naturally."

He continued patiently, breathing deliberately. Slowly, something shifted. His next inhalation felt suddenly electrifying, vibrant energy surging powerfully through him, like lightning flashing unexpectedly through the night sky. His following exhalation resonated deeply within his throat, a whisper echoing quietly, much like distant thunder rolling gently across the horizon.

This imagery unfolded vividly within Daniel's awareness. Each breath cycle became more distinct, more intense, lightning-like energy piercing inward on inhalation, rolling thunder expanding outward on exhalation. Daniel marveled at this vivid sensation, unlike anything he'd experienced before in his meditation practice.

As his session continued, Daniel noticed something curious— the energetic lightning did not always strike downward. Occasionally, it veered suddenly to the left or right, sometimes ascending toward the crown of his head, or spreading outward, unexpected paths dictated by subtle internal shifts he hadn't consciously directed.

Remembering Adrian's advice, Daniel resisted the urge to control these movements, instead simply observing. With each breath, he became increasingly attuned to the subtle factors influencing these energetic directions: slight changes in posture, emotional nuances, fleeting thoughts. Each subtle internal shift reshaped the lightning's trajectory and altered the depth of the thunder's resonance.

The storm outside his apartment intensified, the rain gently tapping against the windows, mirroring Daniel's inner experience. The external storm became an unexpected ally, grounding his meditation and reinforcing the vividness of his breathing practice.

Afterward, Daniel shared his experiences with Adrian, describing the profound sensations and unexpected variations.

"It's remarkable," Daniel explained thoughtfully. "The energy didn't follow a set path—it moved freely, unpredictably. Sometimes upward, sometimes sideways, sometimes radiating outward."

Adrian smiled knowingly. "Exactly. Storm Breathing reveals the dynamic, unpredictable nature of our internal energies. The goal isn't to control the storm, but to witness it fully. In observing without interference, you understand the subtle interplay between breath, body, and mind."

70

Inspired, Daniel deepened his practice over subsequent weeks. Each session revealed new subtleties, deepening his awareness of how emotions, thoughts, and posture influenced the energetic flow. Storm Breathing began transforming not just his meditation practice, but also his everyday experiences. Daniel became more mindful of his internal state, better able to recognize and release tensions before they took hold.

One evening, as Daniel practiced quietly, an especially vivid meditation unfolded. His inhalations crackled vividly with lightning-like clarity, his exhalations resonating profoundly through his body like rolling thunder. In that heightened state, he observed a powerful energetic shift: the internal lightning surged upward through his spine, radiating outward, filling him with profound clarity and calm.

Afterward, he sat quietly, deeply moved by the experience. Storm Breathing had shown him something profound: the incredible power residing within his breath, the subtle yet dynamic interplay between calm lunar inhalations and powerful solar exhalations.

Daniel shared this insight with friends interested in deepening their own practices, guiding them gently through Storm Breathing. They too described vivid experiences, profound inner storms that cleared tension, heightened awareness, and fostered deep emotional release.

Months into his practice, Daniel noticed that Storm Breathing became intuitive, almost second nature. Whether meditating or simply moving through his day, he now effortlessly transitioned between calm lunar breaths and resonant solar breaths, navigating life's storms with newfound ease and clarity.

One afternoon, during a gentle rainstorm, Daniel met Adrian once again, reflecting gratefully on his journey.

"Storm Breathing taught me something powerful," Daniel shared warmly. "Our inner energies are as dynamic as a storm—

sometimes calm, sometimes intense, always shifting. By simply observing these movements without interference, I've learned to find deep peace amidst life's unpredictability."

Adrian nodded with quiet pride. "Exactly, Daniel. You've discovered Storm Breathing's greatest gift—not control, but deep, profound awareness."

As the gentle rain tapped quietly on the window, Daniel closed his eyes briefly, taking a deep, lunar inhale, then exhaling softly through his throat, feeling the familiar, comforting thunder resonate quietly within him.

Storm Breathing had become more than a practice—it had become his guide, teaching him daily to remain grounded amidst life's unpredictable storms, breathing calmly and powerfully, fully present within each moment.

MEDITATION

Foreword

When we meditate using the techniques described so far—mainly combining belly breathing, lunar breathing, and solar breathing—we will begin to experience a variety of signs and sensations that serve as indicators of our progress. These signs are not random occurrences; rather, they are meaningful responses that our body and mind produce as we navigate deeper states of awareness. By paying close attention to these signs, we can learn to interpret them, using them as valuable feedback that reveals how our meditation is influencing our inner world.

To fully grasp these signs, we must refine our ability to visualize and sense the subtle interplay between breath, movement, and mental states. The way air moves through our body is not merely a mechanical function but an intricate expression of our current energetic state. If we allow ourselves to simply observe the breath without interference, it will begin to reveal natural patterns, flowing into different areas of our body and, in some cases, extending beyond the boundaries of our physical form. Understanding the significance of these movements grants us an opportunity to gain insight into our inner nature, illuminating areas of imbalance, harmony, and potential growth. Through this awareness, we can make adjustments not only within our meditation but also in how we carry ourselves through daily life, bringing about profound realizations that shape our perspectives and behaviors.

Although various traditions and symbolic systems provide different frameworks for interpreting these signs, I will outline a foundational set of symbols that can serve as a guide during our practice. These symbols, though simple, can be remarkably effective in helping us navigate the subtle language of the breath and its connection to the five elements of nature and the nine planets of the solar system.

The Five Elements

When the breath flows downward, moving below the chest, we are engaging with the earth element. This downward flow is associated with stability, grounding, and physical awareness. It can indicate a deepening sense of calm and rootedness, as well as a need to establish stronger foundations in life, whether emotional, mental, or material.

Conversely, when the breath rises above the chest, lifting toward the throat and beyond, we align with the air element. This movement is often linked to expansion, mental clarity, and lightness. It may reflect an opening of thought, heightened creativity, or a shift into more subtle, abstract realms of consciousness. A strong upward flow can signify moments of inspiration or transcendence, though an excessive focus in this area may also lead to restlessness or disconnection from the body.

If the breath moves predominantly toward the left side of the body, we are attuning to the water element. This flow embodies fluidity, adaptability, and emotional sensitivity. Water-like breath movements often correspond with the release of emotions, the surfacing of deep-seated feelings, or a heightened sense of intuition. They invite us to embrace change, allowing emotions to flow rather than become stagnant.

On the other hand, when the breath is drawn more intensely to the right side of the body, we engage with the fire element. This directional flow is associated with warmth, energy, and dynamic transformation. A fiery breath pattern can signify motivation, inner strength, and the ignition of willpower. However, if unbalanced, it may also indicate agitation, impatience, or excessive intensity that requires conscious tempering.

Each of these elemental movements contains further layers of meaning, which can be explored by observing the specific sensations and subtle shifts that arise during meditation. By cultivating a refined awareness of these breath patterns, we gain the ability to work harmoniously with our energy, transforming our practice into a tool for both self-discovery and intentional transformation.

The **Earth** element embodies the essence of stability, foundation, and the tangible aspects of existence. It represents grounding, nature, physical health, basic survival needs, material wealth, and everything that is purely physical and material. Just as the earth provides a solid base upon which all life depends, this element serves as the bedrock of our being, supporting both our internal and external worlds. Through it, we connect to the tangible, the practical, and the immediate realities of life—our body, our sustenance, and our sense of security in the physical realm.

Within this element, we can identify three primary areas or energy wheels that correspond to different aspects of our physical and material existence. These areas are interconnected, each playing a vital role in maintaining the overall balance of our being.

The first and most expansive of these areas is the belly region. This zone extends from the base of the chest down to just above the groin, encompassing the stomach, intestines, and digestive organs. It is intimately connected to nourishment, consumption, and the fulfillment of basic needs. This is the center of primal sustenance, where we process food, absorb energy, and regulate many essential bodily functions. On a deeper level, it also represents our desires, our cravings, and the way we seek comfort in the material world. A healthy flow of breath into this region suggests harmony in our ability to receive and process sustenance, while blockages may point to imbalances in our relationship with food, stability, or even emotional security.

The second wheel of the Earth element is found within the area of the sexual organs. This zone governs sexuality, reproduction, and the creative force of life itself. It is linked to passion, intimacy, and the drive for continuation and connection. The breath flowing into this area indicates activity in our sexual and creative energies, illuminating aspects of our desires, attractions, and the way we relate to others on a deeply personal level. It is also where the physical expression of our emotions often takes form, whether through acts of intimacy, the desire for closeness, or the energy of procreation. A well-balanced energy in this space allows for a healthy connection to one's own sexuality and creative impulses, while disruptions may manifest as repression, excessive indulgence, or emotional entanglements.

The third area encompasses the legs and feet, the structures that quite literally support us and allow us to navigate the world. This region is closely tied to survival instincts, movement, and our ability to take action in response to external circumstances. It is where we experience our fight-or-flight response, as well as our relationship with fear, stability, and movement through life. Strong, steady breath into this area can signify groundedness and confidence, while tension or resistance may indicate fear, hesitation, or instability in facing life's challenges.

Beneath these three wheels lies the earth itself—the solid ground upon which we stand, the foundation that upholds our existence. When our breath flows beneath our feet, we connect to the raw, unfiltered essence of the Earth element. This is the most primal and direct link to nature, the force that supports all life, providing a sense of unwavering stability and deep-rooted strength.

It is essential to recognize that the Earth element is not hierarchically inferior to the others. It does not exist as a lower or lesser force but rather as the fundamental structure upon which all else is built. Without it, the other elements—air, fire, and water— would lack the grounding necessary to manifest effectively in our lives. Just as a tree must have strong roots to reach toward the sky, we too must cultivate a strong foundation in order to explore higher aspects of our being. The Earth element is not only the source of our material well-being but also the container that allows transformation, balance, and deeper exploration to take place. By honoring it, we establish a firm footing that enables us to grow, evolve, and ultimately ascend with stability and confidence.

The **Air** element represents the vast and boundless nature of the immaterial world. It is the realm of thought, ideas, abstract concepts, and the ceaseless movement of the mind. Unlike the Earth element, which is rooted in tangible reality, or Water and Fire, which operate along horizontal planes of balance, Air exists in the vertical dimension but is inherently formless, flowing freely between different states of awareness. It is the element of inspiration, intellect, and expansion—where thoughts take flight, where plans are formulated, and where the unseen forces of imagination and creativity emerge.

Within this element, we can identify three primary energy wheels, each corresponding to different mental faculties and cognitive functions. These areas act as the main centers through which the Air element manifests, shaping our perception, understanding, and connection to the intangible aspects of existence.

The first wheel is located at the throat, the seat of communication and verbal expression. This region governs speech, the articulation of thoughts, and the way we interact with others through language. It is the bridge between internal ideas and external reality, allowing us to share, persuade, and connect through words. When the breath moves strongly in this area, it signifies activity in our ability to communicate, whether through speaking, writing, or even unspoken forms of expression such as body language and tone. A well-balanced throat center enables clarity, honesty, and effective articulation, while an imbalance may lead to difficulties in expressing oneself, miscommunication, or excessive verbosity without true meaning.

The second wheel is found at the top of the head, where deeper intellectual processes take place. This is the domain of higher reasoning, abstract thought, and complex mental constructs. It is here that we contemplate philosophical questions, ethical dilemmas, and overarching ideas such as justice, morality, and existential matters. This area does not concern itself with immediate sensory experiences but instead dwells in the realm of analysis, logic, and conceptualization. When breath energy concentrates here, it may indicate a heightened engagement with intellectual pursuits, a surge of critical thinking, or deep contemplation of life's greater questions. However, an imbalance in this center may lead to over-intellectualization, detachment from emotions, or an inability to act upon one's insights.

The third wheel resides in the forehead, where imagination and visualization take shape. This is the realm of creative thought, dreams, and the ability to form mental images of things not yet seen. Here, we process abstract symbols, create artistic visions, and tap into the power of foresight and innovation. A strong presence of breath in this region suggests heightened creativity, visualization skills, and a vivid mental landscape. When in balance, this center allows us to see beyond the immediate and conceptualize new possibilities. However, when unbalanced, it can result in excessive daydreaming, unrealistic expectations, or difficulty distinguishing between imagination and reality.

Above these three wheels lies the final and most expansive region—the sky-wheel, which extends beyond the physical body and into the open vastness above. This is the domain of transcendent thought, where ideas surpass the limits of intellect and logic, venturing into the mysteries that elude rational comprehension. It is the space of deep intuition, spiritual insight, and contemplation of the unknown. Concepts such as life after death, the nature of existence, and cosmic interconnectedness belong to this sphere. When the breath reaches this area, it signals an openness to higher wisdom, moments of profound realization, or a connection to something beyond the self.

The Air element, with its constant movement and limitless scope, is essential for intellectual and creative growth. Yet, just like the wind itself, it must be guided and balanced. When too dominant, it may lead to excessive thinking, disconnection from the physical world, or an inability to remain grounded. When too weak, it can result in stagnation, a lack of inspiration, or difficulty processing abstract ideas. By observing how the breath interacts with these different centers, we gain insight into our mental state and can work toward achieving a harmony between thought, expression, creativity, and higher understanding.

While Earth and Air are often regarded as vertical elements, signifying structure and movement between higher and lower realms, Water and Fire are considered horizontal elements, responsible for balance, distribution, and modulation. These two forces do not move up or down in the same way as Earth and Air; instead, they spread outward, extending laterally through our being, ensuring that energy is neither overly concentrated nor left stagnant. They serve as the counterweights to the vertical elements, ensuring that no single aspect of our existence dominates at the expense of another.

This dynamic becomes apparent when we observe the natural flow of our breath. Even when the breath moves into a specific region, such as the belly area, it rarely remains perfectly centered. More often than not, it will subtly drift to the right or left, carrying with it the influence of either the Water or Fire element. If the breath veers leftward, it signifies the presence of a water-related condition—passivity, adaptability, emotional depth, or introspection. Conversely, if the breath shifts toward the right, it indicates the influence of fire—activity, determination, intensity, or strong-willed passion.

A perfectly centered breath in any given region reflects a state of equilibrium, a moment of inner harmony where neither extreme overpowers the other. This balance does not mean a lack of movement, but rather a dynamic and self-sustaining stability in which both elements are present in equal measure, reinforcing and complementing each other rather than clashing. This is an ideal state, yet one that requires continuous awareness and subtle adjustments to maintain.

Water, as an element, embodies passivity, tranquility, and emotional fluidity. It is the force of reflection, deep contemplation, and calm, flowing emotions. Just as a body of water gently shifts with the wind and contours itself to any shape, this element represents adaptability, patience, and the ability to navigate challenges with grace rather than force. It extends beyond the physical body, reaching outward to the far left, creating a field of energy that influences the way we interact with our emotions, our thoughts, and the world around us. A dominant water influence can bring peace, but if imbalanced, it may lead to excessive detachment, indecision, or an overwhelming tendency toward passivity.

Fire, on the other hand, is the element of activity, intensity, and raw energy. It is the force of passion, drive, and immediate action, infusing life with purpose and determination. Like flames that spread quickly, it represents a sense of urgency, a desire to transform, and the willpower to push forward despite obstacles. This element extends outward to the far right, creating an energetic force field that drives ambition, movement, and intensity in our thoughts and actions. A strong fire element brings vitality, motivation, and confidence, but when unchecked, it can manifest as impulsiveness, aggression, or emotional volatility.

These two forces exist both inside and outside of us, influencing not only our inner states but also the way we interact with the world. While they appear as opposites, they are ultimately interdependent. Fire needs water's cooling presence to prevent it from burning out of control, while water requires fire's warmth and energy to avoid stagnation and inertia. The dance between these elements is a constant interplay, shaping our moods, decisions, and interactions. By becoming more attuned to their influence within our breath and body, we can cultivate a deeper sense of balance, ensuring that neither passivity nor intensity dominates our being, but rather that they work together in perfect harmony.

Even if we achieve harmony among all the elemental areas and their corresponding wheels, true equilibrium is only found within the Spirit Wheel, the central point of all energy, situated in the middle of the chest. Unlike the other elements, which each have their own qualities and functions, the Spirit Element is not tied to any singular force. Instead, it is the symbol of pure, uncorrupted balance, the meeting place where all energies converge in unity.

When any of the four elements—Earth, Water, Fire, or Air—reaches a state of balance, the breath will naturally flow toward the **Spirit** Wheel, drawn to its center like a river returning to the ocean. This phenomenon reflects the deeper truth that harmony within any single aspect of our being inevitably leads to a more profound, overarching sense of peace. However, when all elements are in alignment, when none is overactive or deficient, the breath, regardless of where it originates, will always return to this sacred center. This is where true happiness, clarity, and enlightenment reside, where we experience the highest form of existence—a state of effortless, boundless presence.

Yet, the journey does not end here. Even when the breath is fully centered in the Spirit Wheel, the process of deepening this balance is infinite. With each inhalation, we refine our awareness, with each exhalation, we dissolve into deeper serenity. The experience of this center is not static but ever-expanding, unfolding new layers of bliss, ecstasy, and transcendence as we continue through life. The more we cultivate awareness of this space, the more we realize that harmony is not a destination but a continuous unfolding—a boundless journey toward greater joy, peace, and unity with the essence of existence itself.

Amelia opened her eyes slowly, feeling the warm, gentle embrace of morning sunlight filtering through her curtains. Today felt different. There was a subtle shift within her—a quiet anticipation that resonated deep in her chest. Recently, Amelia had come to understand that her internal experiences during meditation often reflected the nuances of her daily life, revealing the subtle yet profound dance of the Five Elements: Earth, Air, Water, Fire, and Spirit.

On an early spring morning, Amelia found herself planting flowers in her garden. Her hands sank into the rich, damp soil, each careful placement grounding her deeply in the Earth element. She relished the tangible sensations, the scent of freshly turned earth, the quiet satisfaction of physical labor. That evening, as she meditated, Amelia felt her breath naturally descend below her chest, firmly rooting her in a sense of stability and calm. She sensed clearly how her day's grounding activities had manifested internally, creating a profound sense of rootedness within her.

A few days later, an unexpected conversation sparked Amelia's imagination. Over coffee, a friend shared vivid stories of recent travels, igniting Amelia's curiosity and creativity. Her mind soared, filled with images of distant places, ideas for new creative projects blossoming effortlessly. That night, in meditation, Amelia observed her breath rising lightly toward her throat and head, mirroring her heightened intellectual and imaginative state—the unmistakable influence of the Air element. The expansiveness felt inspiring yet delicate, reminding her of Leah's gentle warning that too much Air could create restlessness.

In another moment, Amelia found herself comforting a friend struggling emotionally. Sitting together in quiet empathy, she felt an instinctive openness, allowing herself to be fully present with the complex emotions unfolding between them. Later, as she meditated, Amelia noticed a subtle pull to the left side of her body, her breath softly embodying the Water element. Emotional fluidity enveloped her gently, enabling her to recognize the importance of vulnerability and compassion in her daily interactions.

Conversely, a particularly challenging workday ignited Amelia's fiery resolve. She addressed difficult tasks head-on, navigating intense discussions with clarity and purpose. The decisive actions left her energized and assertive. That evening, her meditation was charged, her breath shifting distinctly to her right side, invoking the powerful, dynamic force of Fire. Amelia recognized the inner strength and motivation that arose naturally from engaging proactively with life's challenges.

Each day's meditation became an intricate reflection of Amelia's life, a mirror revealing her internal state shaped by external experiences. The elements were not just abstract concepts —they were living forces within her, continually influenced by her choices, interactions, and daily activities.

Amelia began noticing subtle shifts during meditation more clearly. A weekend retreat offered a unique opportunity for deeper observation. Surrounded by nature, Amelia alternated between quiet walks, creative writing sessions, heartfelt conversations, and rigorous physical activities. Each experience subtly influenced her breath, guiding it toward different elemental energies.

One quiet afternoon, sitting beneath a sprawling oak tree, Amelia felt an extraordinary sense of balance, her breath settling gently into the center of her chest—the Spirit Wheel. It was as though all elements converged harmoniously, resulting in profound inner peace. In that moment, she deeply understood Leah's teachings: true equilibrium arises from consciously balancing life's diverse activities and recognizing their interplay within one's inner world.

The retreat clarified Amelia's understanding further. She realized the non-linear nature of her experiences; life was not a straightforward journey but a complex, interwoven tapestry. Some days demanded grounding, others creativity or emotional connection, and occasionally, decisive action. Her meditation reflected these shifting needs, offering vital insights into maintaining inner balance.

Back home, Amelia approached life differently. Each interaction and decision was deliberate, mindful of its elemental influence. Hosting a dinner, she intentionally combined grounding Earth energies in preparing nourishing food, stimulating Air in thought-provoking conversations, emotional Water in fostering intimate connections, and dynamic Fire in spirited debates. Her meditation that evening vividly reflected this intentional integration, her breath effortlessly aligning with the Spirit Wheel, highlighting profound inner harmony.

Over weeks, Amelia grew more adept at recognizing subtle imbalances and addressing them proactively. Days filled with excessive intellectual activity prompted grounding exercises or quiet emotional reflection. Periods dominated by intense activity were balanced with restful creativity or solitude. Gradually, Amelia found herself naturally moving toward equilibrium, her daily life thoughtfully balanced by conscious choices.

A particularly enlightening moment came during a challenging period at work. The intense demands led her breath to become overly fiery, causing restlessness and agitation. Recognizing this imbalance, Amelia deliberately integrated more grounding Earth activities and fluid, reflective Water experiences into her routine. She spent evenings gardening, journaling, and meditating, allowing her breath to rebalance naturally toward calm and stability.

Each meditation became an intimate dialogue with herself, revealing insights into her inner state shaped by external realities. Amelia learned to read her breath like a language, interpreting subtle movements as messages from her subconscious. This awareness profoundly impacted her relationships, career choices, and personal development, creating an intentional, fulfilling life.

Months passed, marked by continuous exploration and growth. Amelia understood deeply that meditation wasn't just about inner reflection; it was about cultivating conscious alignment between her external actions and internal energies. The Five Elements guided her, serving as a compass navigating the complexities of daily life.

The Nine Planets

The analogy of the nine planets serves as a next step, after the concept of the five elements has been mastered and refined. The nine planets serve as what we could call an anchor. When we choose one of the planets as an anchor, it means that instead of focusing on our breath, we focus on a concept and let our breath go, allowing it to flow freely where it may, without us necessarily being aware of its direction or shape.

An anchor serves as a point of reference or a focal point around which our meditation practice can be centered. Instead of completely letting go of your awareness or focusing it solely on your breath, you gently "flex" that same "mental muscle" into focusing on a concept. This must be an open focus, not a mental process. It means you attune with the concept you are anchoring to. You need not imagine or think about the concept; simply bring your awareness to it. The more esoteric and immaterial this concept is, the better, since it becomes clear that you are simply trying to connect to this concept and nothing else.

In a way, it might feel like you are not doing anything but keeping your awareness on a concept rather than on a part of your body or your breathing itself. This is a more advanced technique that allows you to get out of the repetitive and somewhat circular motion of breath. By focusing on a non-dual concept, you can transcend the dualities of breath, such as in and out, up and down, left and right. This shift in focus helps to cultivate a deeper sense of unity and oneness, moving beyond the limitations of the physical and mental realms.

To practice using an anchor, find a comfortable seated position with your back straight and your body relaxed. Begin by taking a few deep, diaphragmatic breaths to center yourself. Once you feel settled, choose a planet that resonates with you and that you wish to use as your anchor.

Gently bring your awareness to this concept without trying to think about it or visualize it. Allow your awareness to rest gently on the concept, as if you are simply holding it in your mind's eye. As you do this, let your breath flow naturally and freely, without trying to control it or be aware of its direction or shape. The key is to maintain a soft, open focus on the concept, allowing it to fill your awareness without effort or strain. If done correctly, this practice can be used as a shortcut to gather the breath directly into the spirit wheel situated in the chest area.

The planets referred to in this analogy are the original solar system: Mercury, Venus, Earth, Mars, Jupiter, Saturn, Uranus, Neptune, and Pluto. Each of these planets governs a specific cosmological concept that is key in the functioning of the universe and our existence as human beings.

We can practice all planets or focus on a single anchor that we find most comfortable. In this way, we can direct our breath and energy automatically into our spiritual center and advance rapidly in achieving deep realizations about ourselves, our life, and the universe.

Mercury is the planet of space. The place we are in and all the places in the universe occupy a space. This concept of space is what we would be using as an anchor if we were to choose this planet. Our awareness is drawn to the space that we occupy, the space that surrounds us, and the connection between all physical spaces. When we attune with Mercury, the idea of space as a multidimensional concept begins to unfold, and we are immersed into this universal constant, gathering our consciousness through it, into our spiritual wheel.

*

Rain ticked quietly against the window, a rhythm too precise to be random. Elias sat cross-legged in the near-dark, incense curling upward beside him like language yet to be spoken. Across from him, Selene leaned into the shadows, her profile sharp, eyes bright in the candlelight.

"You ever really feel a room?" she asked, barely above a whisper.

Elias opened one eye. "Feel a room?"

She nodded. "Not the walls or the furniture. The space. The fact that it's here, around you. The fact that it holds you."

He didn't answer right away. Instead, he inhaled, slow and deep, letting the sound of the rain filter through his senses. The air in the room pressed against his skin gently, like a silent presence. There was something there—had always been there—but he hadn't known to listen for it.

"That's the trick," she said, eyes closing. "The space isn't empty. It's not background. It's the stage, the silence before the word, the pause before the note. Everything rides on it."

Elias nodded slowly, beginning to sense it.

They'd been meeting weekly in this borrowed studio. Concrete floor, cracked walls, leftover mirrors from its days as a dance space. But none of that mattered now. What mattered was the invisible shape of the place, how the breath moved in it, how the corners held quiet like secrets.

Selene spoke again, softer now. "Close your eyes. Let yourself fall into the space. Not just the room, but every inch between your skin and everything else."

He obeyed. At first, it was a meditation like any other. Awareness flickering between breath, posture, and the ambient sounds of the world. But something shifted when he stopped looking at things and began looking between them. The silence thickened, became textured.

He could feel the gap between his shoulder and the wall behind him. The invisible arch between his knees and the floor. The entire volume of air that he sat inside like a bubble of awareness.

Then it expanded.

Elias felt his perception stretch—not out of his body, but through the space it occupied. He remained fully present, but now aware of the distance between his cells, the architecture of void that shaped his form.

"Good," Selene murmured, as if reading him from within. "Now step back."

The shift was subtle, like moving behind your own eyes. He wasn't in the room anymore. He was the room. Or rather, he was inhabiting it from a deeper perspective, a vantage point unbound by location.

He saw the space as a web—lines of connection crisscrossing invisibly, weaving the furniture, the bodies, the breath, all into a single tapestry. Every object had its place, and that place resonated. It wasn't random. It couldn't be.

A sudden chill danced down his spine.

"The connection between all places," Selene said, now almost a part of the air. "It's not about going somewhere. It's about understanding that somewhere is already here."

Elias opened his eyes, or thought he did. The room hadn't changed—but it had. Every angle seemed sharper. Every distance more articulate. The silence hummed with structure.

"You're seeing it," Selene smiled. "The shape of space."

He looked around, disoriented but calm. "This isn't just about this room."

"No," she said. "It's about every room. Every field. Every alley. Every rooftop. All the places that ever were and ever could be. They're not separate. They're connected by awareness. Like beads on a thread you didn't know was there."

Elias stood, testing the sensation. His body felt normal, but there was a pull—like gravity—but not to the ground. To position. To location as a presence, not just a coordinate. As he moved, he felt ripples in the room, as though his motion was acknowledged by the space itself.

"Think about it," Selene continued. "What if movement isn't about pushing through space, but shifting your point of reference within a unified whole? What if distance is a perception, not a barrier?"

He turned toward her, mind catching fire. "Then space isn't passive. It's... participatory."

She grinned, pleased. "Exactly. And once you feel that, really feel it, then movement—real movement—can happen without taking a single step."

He thought of old temples, long paths walked with bare feet. Thought of the city's chaos, its compressed distances, the vibration of subways under stone. How every space held a memory, a story, and how those stories hummed at the edges of consciousness.

94

"You're saying awareness is the key," he said.

"No," she corrected gently. "I'm saying awareness is the space."

They stood together in silence. Elias no longer saw the room as walls and air. He saw it as relationship. He saw the hallway beyond, the street, the city skyline hidden behind curtains. And further still—rooms he'd once sat in, places he'd once known. All stitched together through attention, through memory, through some unspoken fabric that stretched infinitely.

"Where does it end?" he asked, awed.

Selene's voice was like wind in the dark. "It doesn't. That's the point."

Outside, the rain had stopped. But the space it had filled remained, echoing like a held breath.

Venus is the planet of life. It governs our living body, animals, trees, plants, and all the life that exists in our world. When using this planet as an anchor, we become aware of the infinite and constant activity of life and the spiritual meaning it carries in our existence as human beings. As with any other anchor, it gathers our consciousness into our spiritual wheel and reveals profound truths about life and its relationship to the universe.

*

The garden didn't belong to her—not in the way people usually mean it. She didn't own it. She didn't plant the twisted olive trees or the low beds of sage and white nettle. But each time Naya stepped through the crooked iron gate, the space folded around her like a welcome she hadn't known she needed. The soil spoke, and she had learned to listen.

It started with silence, always. Not the absence of noise, but a thick, living quiet—like the breath a forest takes before the birds begin to sing.

"Put your feet on the ground," Lucien had told her once, long ago. "Not just on it. Into it."

He'd been the first to teach her. Not the secrets written in books, but the ones rustling in the leaves, pulsing in the stems of weeds most people never noticed.

Today she moved through the garden barefoot. Late sunlight filtered through the branches in shimmering beams, and the air held that momentary stillness that falls just before dusk claims the world.

She knelt beside a dying fern—browned at the edges, curling inward. Most would call it past saving. But Naya had learned that death, in places like this, was rarely final.

She pressed two fingers to its stalk, not to test its strength but to feel its story. Beneath the wilted fronds, life still pulsed—delicate but insistent. She closed her eyes and let her breath fall into rhythm with it.

Everything in the garden breathed. The twisted grapevines along the stone wall. The moss clinging to the fountain's edge. Even the insects nestled beneath bark or inside flower beds were part of the great tide. Life didn't sleep—it moved constantly, cycling, creating, uncreating, renewing.

"Don't meditate on life," Lucien had said once. "Meditate with it."

The memory brought a faint smile.

Naya settled onto the earth, cross-legged, hands open on her knees, and let the world rush in. Not all at once—but as a rising tide, full of heartbeat and whisper.

At first, there was only her own breath, the steady rise and fall of her chest. But then, without effort, she felt another breath underneath it—the breathing of the soil, the plants, the roots twisting in dark silence beneath her. Not metaphor. Not imagery. Reality.

She could feel the song of growth—so slow most people missed it. Sap flowing. Leaves unfolding. Fungal webs spreading through damp loam like invisible nerves. This was the pulse of the green, the language of everything that lives and dies and lives again.

It was in the spiderweb glinting in the corner of the trellis. In the worms turning death into new soil. In her own blood, pushing rhythmically beneath skin and vein.

"This is the anchor," she whispered to no one.

Her awareness was no longer tethered to thought. It drifted effortlessly through the field of life itself, carried by the interconnected hum of being. She could feel the dog barking two gardens over. The shifting of crows settling onto telephone lines. The decaying tree across the street, limbs bare but alive with beetles and larvae. All of it part of the same net, vibrating with one message: You are part of this. You always were.

Lucien had told her once that human arrogance was rooted in disconnection. "We forget that we're just another limb on the body of life," he'd said. "But when you remember—even for a second— you'll see things most people walk past every day and never truly see."

She had tested this, again and again. Once, in a public square, she had sat still and opened herself to the pulse of life amidst concrete and glass. And it was there. In the pigeons pecking at crumbs. In the child laughing into the wind. Even in the homeless man sleeping beneath the scaffolding, breath shallow but steady. Each pulse, each motion, a ripple in the web.

Now, in the garden, she felt something deeper stirring.

The plants around her seemed to lean subtly toward her—not physically, but energetically, the way a flame draws toward oxygen. Not to feed on her, but to include her.

And then—clarity.

It wasn't just awareness of life. It was awareness as life. Her thoughts became less a narrative and more a sensation, as if her consciousness had spilled into the space around her. She was not the observer. She was part of the observed.

A bee landed softly on her wrist. She didn't move. It stood still for a moment, as if verifying her presence, then lifted off again. There was no fear. Only recognition.

This was the truth Venus had revealed: that life is not a separate system we exist inside—it is what we are. Our bodies are gardens. Our minds, ecosystems. Every action, every breath, alters the field.

She felt tears at the edge of her eyes. Not sadness. Not joy. Just the fullness of being—a moment of perfect participation in something far older, and far wiser, than thought.

When Naya opened her eyes, the light had changed. The sun now rested low, casting golden fire through the olive leaves.

She stood slowly, grounding each step with reverence. Around her, the garden shimmered—not with light, but with presence. Nothing had changed. Yet everything had.

In the distance, she could hear children laughing. A car engine rumbled to life. A bird called out once, sharp and clear.

Life, uninterrupted.

She whispered a quiet thank you—not to the garden, but to the field itself. Then she stepped back through the iron gate and into the world, carrying the pulse of the green within her.

Earth is the planet of matter. Rocks, metals, machines, and all inert objects are under the governance of Earth. When using this planet as an anchor, our consciousness is drawn into the spiritual wheel, giving us a deep connection to all matter that exists in the universe. The solidity and presence of material forms become an avenue through which we can ground ourselves in meditation.

*

The warehouse was silent, save for the hum of electricity coursing through steel conduits and the occasional distant creak of settling concrete. Jonas stood still, hands brushing the edge of a rusted workbench, eyes tracing the contours of old machines asleep beneath dust. He came here when he needed to remember.

Not the past. The real—that particular quality of reality that most people mistake for burden. But he had learned better. From the stones, from the iron beams, from the heaviness of things that do not move unless made to.

"They aren't dead," she had told him, that first night beneath the mountain. "They're still. That's different."

Her name was Mira, and she'd once lived in a tiny cabin made from reclaimed stone and salvaged rebar, perched at the edge of a quarry long forgotten by maps. She spoke to the mountain the way others might pray. Quiet, reverent, listening more than speaking.

Jonas hadn't understood at first. He came from a world where matter was something to move through, shape, or overcome. Stone was inert. Metal was silent. Wood was useful. That was all.

Until it wasn't.

He'd arrived at Mira's retreat after a string of restless years— years chasing light, sensation, and air. His mind had been sharp, quick, but untethered. "You don't need more visions," she told him, handing him a hammer. "You need weight."

And so he learned to move stone.

Not in great architectural strokes, but in small, deliberate acts. Lifting. Aligning. Listening.

"Every object carries its own center," she said once, watching him struggle with a slab that refused to sit right. "If you don't honor its balance, it will always resist you."

He hadn't believed her then. But he does now.

Back in the warehouse, Jonas knelt and ran a hand along the floor. Cold. Pitted. Real. The concrete had a presence—it wasn't just where he knelt, it was the kneeling. The act. The choice to stop and be with it.

He settled into meditation, not with breath or mantra, but with posture and contact. Spine aligned with the steel column behind him. Palms flat on the floor. He let gravity speak.

And then it began.

The shift was subtle, always. His awareness, drawn downward —not away, not upward, but inward and down. Into the dense presence of all that held form.

He became aware of the space beneath him—not air, but strata. Layer upon layer of stone, mineral, bone. Earth, ancient and unknowable, pressing upward not to crush, but to witness.

It wasn't visual. It was weight. A kind of communication that bypassed words and spoke in pressure and mass.

He had once meditated on breath, flame, wind, even silence. Each had its own texture. But Earth… Earth was different. It didn't shimmer or flow. It anchored. It invited stillness, but not inaction. A waiting stillness. A poised potential. The way a mountain waits—not because it is lazy, but because it already is.

Mira used to say that matter doesn't ask to be understood. It asks to be respected.

And in return, it teaches.

Jonas exhaled, slowly. His hand brushed a nearby piece of scrap—an old gear, stained with oil and time. In its presence, he felt a whisper—not of speech, but of use. The tool had memory. Not emotional memory, but functional memory. Purpose encoded in its shape. That too was sacred.

The machines here, the tools, the rusted bolts and steel beams —they weren't dead. They were part of the great wheel of solidity. Their silence held a presence more profound than most human noise.

His awareness dropped further.

Down into the molecules of his own body—the bones that mirrored stone, the blood rich with iron, the tissues held in gravity's embrace. He was not a mind inside a body. He was a structure. A shape. A vessel of matter, conscious through material.

And in this alignment, something opened.

Not a vision. Not an epiphany. But a settling. The way dust settles after a storm. The way a heavy bell comes to rest after it rings.

In that place, he remembered what Mira had said when he'd asked her about transcendence.

"You don't transcend the material world," she said. "You honor it. You inhabit it so fully that the boundary between body and world disappears."

She had shown him a piece of basalt once—nothing special, just a rock from the garden. But she held it like a scripture.

"This has endured pressure you can't imagine," she said. "Heat, depth, compression. And still, it holds its form."

Now, in the quiet of the warehouse, Jonas felt that same strength in his own spine.

Not defiance. Not resistance. Just presence.

And in that presence, he understood something deeper: that Earth wasn't here to trap him. It was here to hold him. That matter wasn't his enemy—it was his witness. The keeper of memory, form, and truth. The bones of reality.

Slowly, he opened his eyes.

Nothing had changed.

Everything had.

The machines were still broken. The light still flickered. But Jonas could feel the deep rhythm beneath it all. The spiritual wheel that didn't spin in air or ether, but pulsed through the physical—the touchstone of all that is.

He stood and bowed his head—not to a god, but to the space around him. The weight of iron. The grain of concrete. The stillness that had taught him more than any vision ever could.

He didn't need to seek higher planes.

He was already standing on one.

Mars is the planet of forces. Lightning, igniting fire, gravity, explosions, and other bursts of energy are all related to Mars. Using this planet as an anchor means attuning to the raw, dynamic forces that drive change and movement in the universe. Our awareness becomes sensitive to the undercurrents of force that shape our reality, allowing us to harness this energy in our meditation practice.

*

The substation buzzed.

Not metaphorically—actually. Jonas could hear it from fifty feet away. That electric hum, low and steady, like the breath of something alive but trying not to draw attention to itself. Most people would walk past it without a second thought. But Jonas paused at the fence, one hand resting on the chain links, the other adjusting the strap of his tool bag.

"Don't trust anything that's still but holding voltage," his grandfather had once told him. "Still doesn't mean safe."

He didn't know it back then, but his grandfather had been speaking truth that ran deeper than wires and volts.

Jonas came here sometimes—not to fix, not to study, but to listen.

There was a way the air thickened around places like this. A charge that didn't come from imagination. The turbines, transformers, and lines pulsed with a contained tension. The potential for movement. The kind of power that didn't need permission to change everything in an instant.

He ducked through the gate with the quiet confidence of someone who knew how to stay invisible. Past the switch cabinets, past the metal stairs. He made his way to the heart of the structure —a space shielded from wind and noise, where the great coils sat like coiled serpents, vibrating just below the threshold of perception.

He sat, cross-legged on cold concrete, not for comfort, but for clarity.

And then he breathed.

It wasn't the kind of breath you use to calm yourself. It was the kind that fed the fire. Deep, sharp, precise. Air in, pressurized. Air out, controlled release. Like bellows feeding a forge.

This was not peace-seeking meditation.

It was contact.

He'd learned years ago—under storm-heavy skies, on train tracks, near engines pushing themselves to their limits—that there was a different rhythm to follow when listening to force. Not the flow of air or the settling of bones. But the rising pulse of momentum before the strike.

He had once meditated in an abandoned railyard, where rusted locomotives whispered their old violence. Another time, at the edge of a demolition site, feeling the countdown like a heartbeat in the concrete. Mars, he'd come to call it—not the planet, but the principle.

Force.

Not anger. Not rage. Force. The will that breaks inertia. The breath between spark and explosion. The pressure behind all becoming.

He felt it now.

The substation's coils throbbed with it. Not just electricity—but the possibility of electricity. Of voltage breaking through containment. Of light erupting into form.

Jonas dropped into the space between seconds.

There, his awareness sharpened—not floaty or diffuse, but focused to a point.

It was like becoming a blade. Every breath a hammer strike. Every moment, refined. His mind didn't wander. It drilled.

He didn't dissolve into the environment. He merged with its tension.

In that tension, he could feel it—the forces around him. Gravity pulling his body down. Friction resisting his breath. The pushback of electromagnetic fields. The subtle heat of moving ions in the air.

They weren't just background phenomena. They were participants in a conversation. And they had mass, velocity, charge. They were alive.

He remembered the first time he saw lightning up close—not from a distance, but in the exact moment it struck the iron railing three feet in front of him on a rooftop. The sound had split the air in half. For hours afterward, he couldn't speak. Not because of fear. But because he had understood something. Something about reality's willingness to rupture. To remake itself.

That's what Mars taught.

Not how to stay still.

But how to recognize the moment just before everything moves.

In meditation, Jonas had learned to sit with the arc of that moment. To trace the ignition of fire in his chest, the sudden surge of adrenaline, the tremor in his muscles before they acted. These were not distractions. They were the raw data of change.

The body itself was a chamber of combustion. Blood surged. Neurons fired. Muscles twitched in readiness. Even thoughts arrived as pulses—electric, chemical, kinetic.

Jonas reached into that current now—not with his hands, but with his breath.

A single inhalation pulled his awareness through the coils of the station, through the copper wires, into the grid. He could feel the distant tremble of an entire city's demand. Traffic lights flicking. Elevators shifting. Heaters groaning to life as dusk fell. All of it: force negotiating with resistance.

And all of it mirrored within him.

His spine straightened.

His heart slowed—not in calm, but in control.

He didn't want to be the lightning.

He wanted to be the stormcloud choosing when to release.

That was the lesson Mira had once tried to teach him in the desert, watching a fire she'd built from scratch. "Don't mistake energy for impulse," she said. "The match is nothing. The friction that knows when—that's mastery."

He didn't fully understand her then. But now, in the belly of the substation, he did.

Mars wasn't about violence.

It was about activation.

When to push.

When to break.

When to become more than potential.

Jonas opened his eyes.

His skin tingled. The back of his neck hummed.

But there was no chaos, no wild surge of emotion. Just a kind of luminous readiness.

The meditation ended not with a whisper, but with the quiet gravity of decision.

He stood slowly, every muscle deliberate.

As he left, he looked once more at the humming coils and wires.

They didn't bow. They didn't speak.

But he could feel their acknowledgment—like heat rising through stone long after the fire has gone.

The force was still there.

Waiting.

And so was he.

Jupiter is the planet of magic. Miracles, the esoteric, unseen forces at play, greater unknowns, and mystical knowledge are all related to Jupiter. By choosing this planet as an anchor, we align our awareness with the hidden aspects of existence—the forces that operate beyond logical explanation. This connection allows for deep spiritual insight and an expanded perspective of the universe's mysteries.

*

He wasn't sure why he turned down that alley.

It didn't appear on the map. Didn't follow the geometry of the city. It curved where the grid said it should be straight. It narrowed when it should have widened. Still, Elias walked down it, steps slow, quiet, as if something had already answered a question he hadn't yet asked.

Above, the buildings bent slightly inward, their windows blank like shuttered eyes. The air shimmered—not with heat, but with the strange liquidity of a dream half-remembered. And somewhere in the distance, there was music. Not the kind with instruments. The kind with intention.

Elias had followed hunches before. In his line of study— private, internal, inconveniently real—intuition had long since ceased being a poetic concept. It had become a faculty. Like sight. Like hearing.

He reached a door. Heavy wood. No handle. Just a faint sigil carved at its center—worn smooth by time or fingers.

He placed his palm on it.

The door opened without a sound.

The room inside should not have fit in the alley.

Vaulted ceilings traced with constellations that pulsed in slow rhythm. A long table set with items that refused fixed form: a scroll that sometimes looked like a book, a chalice that flickered between metal and crystal. Candles burned in the wrong direction —wax rising upward from flame.

And at the head of the table, a woman waited.

She wore no robe. No talisman. Just a gray coat and eyes that had seen the structure behind things.

"You heard the call," she said.

Elias nodded slowly. "Didn't know I had."

"You don't need to. Jupiter calls in layers."

He stepped forward. "What is this place?"

She gestured. "A space aligned with what lies just behind the veil of knowing. Here, the symbols move closer to their meanings. But not too close. They still have room to breathe."

Elias moved to the table. He glanced at the chalice. Its surface held reflections he didn't recognize. Not other places. Other possibilities.

"Why now?" he asked. "Why me?"

The woman tilted her head slightly, not unkindly. "Because you've begun to notice that the world is thicker than it seems. That cause and effect only explain half the picture. You're asking the right questions—without trying to carve them into answers."

She stood. The room dimmed, though no light had changed.

"This is the anchor of Jupiter," she said. "Not a place of control. A place of awe. You align with it by surrendering the need to know, and letting yourself see anyway."

Elias felt a pulse behind his eyes—not painful, but wide. Like a door in his perception opening just a crack.

"You think magic is fire and symbols," she continued. "Sometimes it is. But more often, it's silence where there should be *sound. Synchronicity that interrupts coincidence. The feeling that you've been here before in dreams you never remembered."*

She touched the air. A ripple moved outward, invisible but undeniable. The stars above shifted, rearranged themselves into a pattern that made no sense—but felt true.

"The world runs on more than physics," she said. "There are laws deeper than gravity. Threads finer than time. Jupiter governs those. The mysteries. The systems behind systems."

Elias sat.

He didn't speak.

Not because he was afraid, but because words felt like breaking something delicate.

The woman sat too. The table between them held no food. Only presence.

"You don't need to do anything," she said. "Only allow."

He exhaled.

And allowed.

The ripple returned. Inside him this time. Like a wheel turning behind his thoughts.

He felt the pieces shift—the certainties loosening, the spaces between beliefs growing wider.

He saw a child lifting a rock and finding a symbol carved beneath it.

A dying man smiling at a stranger he had never met, saying, "I remember you."

A crow flying in perfect figure-eights over a city rooftop.

He saw these things not as metaphors, but as messages.

He saw that the universe spoke. Not in words. In patterns. In echoes.

Jupiter wasn't the force causing things. Jupiter was the field in which cause and effect fell apart—and reassembled in new configurations. Beyond logic. Beyond linearity. But not beyond meaning.

"People mistake chaos for randomness," the woman said gently. "But chaos has structure. It's just too big to be mapped."

She leaned in, her voice lower now. "You've felt it, haven't you? Those moments when the world seems to look back at you."

Elias nodded.

"The sudden knowing before the event. The number that keeps repeating. The dream that tells you something no one else could know."

"Yes."

"That's Jupiter's breath. It doesn't speak plainly. But it's always speaking."

Elias touched the scroll/book/thing before him. It pulsed beneath his fingers. Not with heat—but with invitation.

He didn't open it.

He didn't need to.

Some knowledge didn't live in pages. It lived in readiness.

And he was ready now.

He stood, the air around him feeling subtly denser—like the atmosphere of a deep forest, rich with things unseen but fully present.

The woman smiled. "When you leave here, you'll still be in the world. But it won't be the same world."

He nodded.

"Because now you'll notice," she said. "The flickers. The winks between things. The shape of questions too strange to answer."

She reached out and touched his forehead, once.

No light. No sound.

Just a deep resonance. Like something ancient and alive recognizing itself.

Then the room faded.

The alley returned.

Quiet. Empty.

Elias stood still for a long time. The city hummed around him, unaware.

But he saw it now.

The undercurrents.

The geometry behind accidents.

The rhythm in the silence.

And he walked forward—not toward certainty, but toward the mystery that had always been watching.

Saturn is the planet of fate. Destiny, chance, randomness, statistics, and probability all fall under Saturn's governance. When using Saturn as an anchor, we attune to the rhythms of destiny, observing the patterns that weave through our lives. This practice leads to an understanding of life's unfolding nature, helping us cultivate acceptance and wisdom in the face of uncertainty.

*

There was a corner table at the old café on Ninth and Alder—one nobody ever seemed to claim.

People passed it over without realizing. Tourists gravitated toward the window seats. Locals chose the booths by the wall. But that small, slightly crooked table in the back? It waited.

Marin had noticed it six times before she finally sat there. Each time she visited the café, that table had been empty—at different hours, on busy days and quiet mornings alike. Always waiting. Not just available, but expectant.

So one rainy Thursday afternoon, she chose it.

No book. No laptop. Just a notebook, half full of dreams she didn't yet know were real.

She ordered a tea and sat, letting her eyes follow the rain trailing sideways down the glass. People came and went. Some smiled. Some argued. Some stared into nothing as if expecting answers to arrive.

Time passed oddly at this table. Not slow, but stretched. Elastic. She found herself remembering things she hadn't thought of in years—a man on a bus with a broken wristwatch. A woman at a market who gave her change before she paid. A coin toss from childhood that somehow led to a move across the country.

And then, the woman arrived.

She didn't introduce herself. She didn't need to.

She wore black, but not like mourning. Like elegance forgotten. Her eyes were sharp—not piercing, but precise. As if they were used to reading threads that others couldn't see.

"You've found the place," she said, as if that were the point.

Marin raised an eyebrow. "What place?"

The woman gestured to the air. "The still point. The axis where the pattern crosses itself."

Marin blinked. "You mean the table?"

"I mean the moment," the woman said. "It just so happens to wear the shape of a table today."

There was a pause—not uncomfortable. Just filled with something vast.

"I don't believe in fate," Marin said finally.

The woman smiled faintly. "That's because you mistake it for control. Most people think fate means things are fixed. That's not what it is. Fate is rhythm. Probability with a pulse."

Marin frowned. "So... like statistics?"

"Exactly. But deeper. Behind every outcome, there are a million paths. Fate is the tension in those paths. The pull toward one over another. Sometimes it's a whisper. Sometimes it's a shove."

Outside, someone dropped a glass. The sound fractured the air like breaking ice. Neither woman flinched.

"You've felt it," the woman said softly. "The pattern. The way things repeat when they shouldn't. The same numbers showing up. The improbable string of accidents that somehow makes a straight line."

Marin didn't answer. She didn't need to.

"You call it coincidence," the woman continued. "But that's just the name you give to moments you're not ready to understand."

There was no arrogance in her tone. Only clarity.

Marin stared down at her tea. The steam curled like smoke signals, forming and reforming shapes she almost recognized.

"Why me?" she asked.

"Because you sat at the table."

"That can't be all."

"It's never all," the woman said. "But it's enough."

She reached into her coat and pulled out a simple object: a silver thread, barely visible, coiled around a thin piece of obsidian.

"This is yours," she said.

Marin didn't take it.

"Not yet," the woman said, placing it on the table between them. "You'll know when."

The thread shimmered, catching no light yet somehow gleaming. It vibrated softly, like it remembered music.

"This isn't fortune telling," the woman said. "It's fortune listening. The thread doesn't tell you where to go. It tells you where things lean. The directions reality prefers."

Marin looked at the thread. "What happens if I follow it?"

"Nothing guaranteed," the woman replied. "Only possibilities. Fate is not promise. It's potential. But if you learn to listen, you'll move through life as if dancing with something ancient."

The rain stopped.

The woman stood.

"I won't see you again," she said. "But the thread will."

And with that, she stepped away—and vanished between blinks.

Marin stared at the thread.

It pulsed once.

She didn't take it that day.

But she returned the next. And the day after. And one morning, without thinking, she reached for it—not out of certainty, but out of alignment.

She began to notice things.

Not grand visions. Subtleties. The tone in someone's voice that told her more than their words. The missed train that led to the chance encounter. The sense that if she paused at just the right moment, life would open.

She didn't always follow the thread. That wasn't the point.

But when she did, the world hummed—like clicking into place.

And over time, she understood:

Fate wasn't a path drawn in stone.

It was a wind. A pull.

It didn't command. It invited.

And those who learned to feel it, not force it, lived not with certainty—but with grace.

Because Saturn doesn't promise safety.

It offers wisdom.

And Marin, day by day, was learning to listen.

Uranus is the planet of death. Decay, rot, disease, corruption, and finality are all associated with Uranus. By anchoring our awareness to Uranus, we confront the impermanence of all things. This practice allows us to develop a deeper understanding of endings, transformation, and the cycle of existence, ultimately leading to an acceptance of the transient nature of life.

*

The gate was open, though no one had passed through in hours.

Amara stepped in quietly, the rusted hinges creaking a soft lament behind her. The air carried a weight—a stillness not of peace, but of presence. Everything in the garden had long since ceased to grow, yet none of it was gone. The leaves, brown and curled, clung to twisted stems. The soil was dry, but not empty. It held something beneath the surface—waiting.

She didn't come here to mourn. She came to remember. And to listen.

The garden belonged to no one. Or perhaps it belonged to everyone who had once tried to flee what it now held. In the city, people had begun to whisper about it—an overgrown yard behind a forgotten house, where plants no longer bloomed but never disappeared. The place where time slowed down and silence deepened.

Amara had found it on a day when the world felt too loud. That was a year ago. She hadn't understood then. Now, she came regularly, as if returning to an old teacher who spoke few words but taught in unflinching truths.

Today, she walked between brittle stalks of flowers she once could have named. They no longer offered color or scent, only form—parched, curled, preserved in a moment long past. There was something beautiful in their refusal to vanish completely.

She found her usual place, a stone bench cracked down the middle. Moss had begun to claim the fracture. She ran her fingers over it, gently, as one might trace an old scar on a beloved face.

"You came back," said a voice.

It wasn't a surprise.

He always came when she sat long enough.

The figure stood across the garden path, beneath a gnarled tree whose bark had split to reveal hollow wood. He was draped in dark wool, heavy despite the warmth in the air. His face was unreadable, not hidden, just still—like marble that had once moved.

"I always do," Amara said.

He nodded once. "Then you're beginning to understand."

She looked around. "Nothing changes here."

"Not in the way you're used to," he replied. "But everything changes."

She watched the ground. Ants moved through the dried veins of a leaf. Fungus bloomed beneath the base of a fallen stem. The wind shifted a piece of bark, revealing a nest of beetles feeding in slow, silent labor.

Decay. Motion without flourish. The other side of growth.

She breathed deeply.

"This is Uranus," the man said softly. "Not the god of lightning or revolution. Not here. Not now. This is the face no one wants to meet. The dissolver. The teacher of endings."

She nodded. "I used to fear death."

"You still do."

"Yes," she admitted. "But not the same way."

125

He sat across from her, on the earth. No ceremony. No drama. Just the sound of their breath between the sighs of a dying garden.

"Everyone wants transformation," he said. "No one wants to rot."

Amara closed her eyes.

When she was younger, she'd believed in transcendence. Light. Ascent. The upward path. But that belief cracked the year her sister died slowly, a body breaking down cell by cell, while her soul remained awake for every moment. That year taught her more than any sermon or spell.

She hadn't come to this garden to escape. She came to anchor herself.

"What you call decay," he said, "is not destruction. It's digestion. Reclamation."

He reached down, pulled up a handful of soil, let it fall through his fingers.

"This," he said, "was once everything."

She looked at the soil. Saw the crushed shells of beetles. The flecks of petal and root. Saw her own hand tremble.

"Why anchor to this?" she asked. "Why meditate on death?"

"Because you are dying too," he said. "In every breath. In every cell."

He leaned closer, voice low. "And because until you learn to sit with endings, you will not truly live."

She felt something inside her body—tight and long-held—begin to exhale. A grief she hadn't noticed unclenched its fist.

"You think your fear is natural," he said. "It isn't. You've been taught to turn away. But there is no separation. Life is death.

Death is life. They are not opposites. They are neighbors. Lovers. Threads woven together."

Amara opened her hands.

She let herself feel it—not the idea of death, but the constant presence of ending. Her own body, aging. The thoughts that would never return. The people she'd lost, not to tragedy, but to time.

In the silence, she began to sense it: not absence, but continuity.

The way an old leaf nourishes new roots. The way silence deepens song.

The garden wasn't dead. It was mid-conversation. Ingesting. Re-forming. Becoming.

The man stood. "You don't need to accept death," he said. "You only need to witness it."

She nodded. Her cheeks were wet. She hadn't realized she'd cried.

"Will I see you again?" she asked.

He smiled, faintly. "Every time you let go."

Then he was gone.

No flash. No whisper. Just an absence that folded back into the garden.

Amara stood. Around her, nothing bloomed. And yet, everything waited.

She placed her hand on the cracked stone one last time, then turned back through the gate.

The wind lifted a few petals into the air—dry and light as dust—and they danced for a moment before settling, as if remembering the shape of wings.

Neptune is the planet of spirits. The traces of consciousness left behind in seemingly inert objects or deceased people, as well as the subtle imprints they still leave on this plane, are all connected to Neptune. Using this planet as an anchor immerses us in the awareness of the unseen echoes of existence, guiding us to perceive the spiritual imprints that shape our world.

*

There was a house on the edge of the city where nothing ever stayed broken.

If a clock stopped ticking, it would tick again days later—no one winding it. If a mirror cracked, the fracture would be gone by morning. The ivy, which had once withered in a winter frost, grew back overnight with strange blue-tinged leaves.

Nico had never seen anyone enter or leave.

But he had watched the lights flicker on at dusk, soft and golden, despite the house being uninhabited for over a decade. Local kids called it haunted. Some said it fed on memories. Others swore they heard whispers if they passed too close to the windows at night.

Nico didn't believe in ghost stories. But he believed in presence. And that house —empty or not—watched.

He came alone, on the first fogged morning of November, carrying only a notebook and a single brass key left behind by someone who used to know things.

The door opened with a sound like breath.

Inside, the air felt thick, but not with dust. More like it was full of things just outside the range of hearing. The silence wasn't empty. It was full of everything that had ever been said there.

The house wasn't grand. Narrow hallway, warped floors, furniture draped in white. But the light—yes, the light—moved like it remembered who once sat beneath it.

Nico walked slowly, each step chosen, each breath an invitation. He wasn't looking for poltergeists or wailing spirits. What he sought couldn't be photographed or measured.

He entered the drawing room. The air shifted around him.

It was here that he felt it most clearly.

Not fear.

Recognition.

As though the space had already memorized his shape, as though it had been waiting.

He sat on the floor. Closed his eyes. Let his thoughts drift, not away from the room, but into it.

He wasn't new to this. His practice had evolved past guided breathwork and posture. He worked with anchors. And today, his anchor was Neptune.

He drew his awareness outward—not to what was visible, but to what lingered behind the visible. The traces. The spiritual sediment.

Every room, he believed, had a memory.

But this one had personality.

He could feel it rising now—just beneath perception. The way a scent clings to clothing, or a voice echoes long after it's gone.

There had been laughter here. Once. He could feel it. Not as a sound, but as a texture. A soft warmth in the walls. Something kind.

But also grief. Heavy. Settled into the floorboards like oil. Not recent, not raw—but deep. Accepted.

And love—complex, layered, unfinished.

None of it came as vision. Just presence.

Neptune, he had learned, didn't show you spirits in the way of horror films or children's stories. It immersed you in memory that didn't belong to you. It revealed the grooves worn into reality by emotion, thought, and lingering will.

And that's what this house was.

A vessel of echoes.

Nico opened his eyes.

The light in the room had changed. Or rather, revealed itself. Dust particles danced like motes of static. The shadows were too still. Everything was charged with meaning.

He stood and walked to a small writing desk. It was closed. He didn't open it.

Instead, he placed a hand on it—and felt the imprint.

A woman. Sitting late at night. Writing letters never sent. Her presence faint, but unmistakable. He could feel her rhythm. The tension in her hand. The words that carried too much weight to be spoken aloud.

Nico whispered, "You stayed."

Not expecting an answer. But something inside the desk shifted slightly. A recognition.

He moved through the house like that—room to room—following the threads of subtle residue. In the bathroom, he felt shame—an old kind. Tied to skin, to aging, to quiet regret.

In the stairwell, he felt playfulness. A child once climbed those steps with a wooden sword, chasing shadows he imagined were dragons.

Every space hummed with something left behind.

This was Neptune's domain.

Not the spirits who had refused to pass on—but the traces of those who had passed through. The impressions left like fingerprints on glass, long after the fingers were gone.

He stood finally in the attic.

Low ceiling. Bare boards. One broken chair.

Here, the feeling was strong.

A final moment. A letting go.

He sat again.

Let Neptune speak.

He saw—without seeing—a man, slumped and still, surrounded by silence. But the silence wasn't empty. It was full of decision. Acceptance. Sorrow held like something precious.

There were no words. No haunting. Only presence.

Neptune didn't demand worship. It asked for witnessing.

And Nico had learned to witness without judgment.

He sat in that quiet, and in doing so, became part of the house's memory. Another layer. Another echo. A soft imprint left behind for whoever might come next.

Eventually, he rose. Walked back down the stairs. Past the hall. To the door that waited patiently.

Outside, the fog had lifted.

The world continued.

Cars moved. Birds called. Children laughed.

But inside him, something had shifted.

Not broken.

Just softened.

Attuned.

Because now, he saw the world differently—not in ghosts or phantoms, but in impressions. In the way a bench still remembered a long conversation. In the way a room seemed sad after someone left it. In the quiet of forgotten places, rich with unseen stories.

Nico stepped back into the street, carrying no proof.

Only presence.

And Neptune, whispering just behind his thoughts, like breath on glass.

Pluto is the planet of time. The past, present, and future—whether linear or circular—fall under Pluto's domain. By choosing Pluto as an anchor, we become attuned to the fluidity of time. Our perception shifts, allowing us to experience time not just as a sequence of moments but as an interconnected whole. This meditation reveals the timeless nature of our awareness.

*

The shop didn't advertise. No sign, no name—just an etched brass symbol above the door, tarnished with age and shaped like an open circle spiraling inward. People walked by without seeing it, the way one might glance past an old lamppost or the leaning edge of a building too narrow to notice.

But Elian noticed.

He had seen it in a dream once—half-forgotten, thick with fog. A ticking sound had followed him through that dream, steady and ancient, not mechanical but inevitable. And so when he passed the alley where the dream had led him, he followed without hesitation.

The door opened soundlessly. Inside, the air felt both ancient and untouched, like the first second of a forgotten century. The scent of oil and wood shavings floated under a veil of dust. Gears hung on the walls like frozen constellations. Every inch of the shop ticked—not loudly, but intimately, like a collective whisper keeping the world aligned.

A man stood behind a glass counter, bent slightly with age but bright in the eyes. He didn't ask Elian what he wanted.

"You came," he said, as though this had already been discussed.

Elian didn't speak. He stepped deeper into the room, feeling it shift beneath his feet.

There were clocks of every kind—grandfather, pocket, digital, even sundials. Some ticked in rhythm. Others ticked against it.

One pendulum swung slowly forward, paused mid-air, and then reversed its arc without completing the motion. Time here was not obeyed—it was presented.

The man gestured to a chair without looking. "You'll want to sit before it begins."

Elian obeyed.

No ritual. No chant. Just stillness.

He let himself drop inward.

He was not new to the practice. He had anchored to air, to life, to force. But today, the thread he followed led downward—into time. Not into memory, exactly, but into the fabric that memory moved through.

Pluto.

He had read the term in a book older than the building it rested in. Not the planet. Not the god. The principle.

Time, in its totality.

Not just the ticking seconds.

But the whole of it.

Now, sitting among the ticking relics, he began to feel it shift.

First, it was his breath. Then, the temperature. Then, the light.

And then, it began to unfold.

He was in the room—but not.

He saw himself sitting. And standing. And entering.

Not reflections.

Moments.

Layered.

Transparent.

All the versions of himself that had ever passed through this space—one from now, one from an hour later, one from a time he hadn't lived yet.

The clocks pulsed. Not synchronized, but harmonious.

This was not linearity. This was co-presence.

Time, here, was not a road. It was a web. And he, in stillness, became the center of the web—not by effort, but by surrender.

The man behind the counter was younger now. And older. And not there at all.

Elian blinked—and found himself in the same chair, but in a different light. Candlelight. A storm outside. A woman stood where the man had been. She was tracing runes into the condensation on the windowpane, her eyes distant.

"She's remembering you," said a voice behind him.

He turned.

It was the man again—but now he held a mirror instead of a clock.

"She remembers you before she meets you," the man said gently. "That's the trick of Pluto. Memory and prophecy are the same mirror. You just see different faces."

Elian's breath caught. Not from fear, but from vastness.

He stood. The room was the same, and entirely changed.

Every clock now told a different kind of time.

One beat with the pulse of a birth.

One slowed with the last breath of someone dying far away.

One ticked only when he remembered something vividly.

And the largest one—the one mounted above the back wall—wasn't ticking at all. It watched.

Elian stepped closer.

It was made of black glass, reflecting no light. And as he stared into it, he saw everything.

Not in detail.

But in continuity.

His childhood steps across the ocean-wet boardwalk. The tremble in his hands the day he said goodbye. The ache in his chest when he opened a letter he never expected. The warmth in his spine when he stood in sunlight after grief.

It was all there.

Not as history.

But as truth.

All of it had already happened. And not happened. And was happening now.

The glass vibrated softly. A hum of something too large to name.

Pluto was not a teacher of beginnings or endings.

Pluto was the wheel itself.

He stepped back, breath steady, tears quiet on his cheek.

The man returned.

"You saw it."

Elian nodded.

"Do you understand now?" the man asked.

Elian didn't answer. Because understanding was too small a word. He had known.

The man smiled.

"That's the gift. Time is not what you follow. It's what follows you."

Elian blinked again.

The chair was empty.

The man was gone.

The clocks ticked.

The shop was quiet.

And time was—everywhere.

He stepped outside. The sky was the same. But the wind felt older. Or maybe he felt younger.

He checked his watch. The hands pointed to a time that no longer felt relevant.

Because now, when he looked at a moment—he no longer saw it as now.

He saw it as always.

And that made all the difference.

The Sun

The Sun could be seen as an analogy for the ultimate divine principle—the source from which all things emanate and to which all things return. It represents not only the physical sustainer of life but also the radiant presence that illuminates all existence. When we use the Sun as an anchor in meditation, we are not focusing on an external celestial body, nor are we visualizing it as a physical entity. Rather, we are attuning our awareness to the essence of divine consciousness—the boundless, omnipresent force that many traditions refer to as God, the Absolute, the Supreme Reality, or the One.

This practice transcends religious and cultural boundaries. It is not confined to a single theological interpretation but rather aligns with any spiritual path that acknowledges an underlying unity to all existence. Whether it be the concept of Brahman in Hinduism, the Tao in Taoism, the Ain Soph of Kabbalah, or the uncreated light of Hesychasm, all these traditions point toward an ultimate reality that is beyond form, yet the source of all form. The Sun, in this sense, is not merely a metaphor but an experiential gateway into divine communion.

By choosing the Sun as an anchor, we undertake what could be considered the final step in any spiritual journey—the direct and unmediated alignment with the divine. Unlike the previous planetary anchors, which focus on specific aspects of existence (space, life, matter, forces, magic, fate, death, spirits, and time), the Sun represents the totality. It is the principle that governs all other principles, the light that gives life to all lesser luminaries.

Just as the Sun is the central force keeping the planets in orbit, God is the unifying presence that sustains all spiritual and material realities. By anchoring our awareness to the Sun, we no longer focus on fragmented aspects of existence but on the source itself.

This practice shifts us from perceiving ourselves as separate beings toward recognizing our oneness with the divine.

The results of this practice, though unique to each practitioner, often mirror the deep mystical states described across various traditions:

A Radiant Heart – Many traditions speak of an inner illumination experienced when the heart fully opens to divine presence. In Christian mysticism, this is often described as the *Sacred Heart*, a state of burning love that consumes all that is false, leaving only pure devotion. In Sufi practice, it is known as *Fana*, the annihilation of the self into divine love. Those who meditate deeply on the Sun often describe a similar phenomenon —a warmth at the center of their being that gradually expands until it fills them completely.

Union with the Light – In esoteric traditions, spiritual enlightenment is often depicted as merging with divine light. The Buddhist concept of *Clear Light* meditation, the Kabbalistic experience of *Divine Radiance*, and the Christian notion of *Theosis* all describe a state where the practitioner no longer perceives themselves as separate from the light. When meditating on the Sun as an anchor, many describe a dissolution of personal identity, as if they are no longer an individual gazing at the light but have *become* the light itself.

Silence Beyond Thought – The highest spiritual states often go beyond imagery and form, leading to a deep silence where all conceptual distinctions dissolve. In Advaita Vedanta, this is called *Turiya*, the fourth state of pure awareness. In Zen, it is *Satori*, an immediate realization beyond words. When using the Sun as an anchor, one eventually reaches a point where even the concept of the Sun dissolves, leaving only presence—silent, infinite, and ungraspable.

Divine Protection and Guidance – Many who practice this form of meditation report an increased sense of divine protection. Just as the Sun in our solar system provides warmth, energy, and life, anchoring to divine consciousness brings a profound sense of inner security. Obstacles seem to dissolve, synchronicities increase, and intuition sharpens. This is often described in mystical traditions as being "guided by the light" or "walking in divine grace."

A Centered and Effortless Life – The ultimate fruit of this practice is a life aligned with divine will. The struggles and resistances of the ego diminish, and one moves through life effortlessly, guided by an inner harmony. This is akin to the Daoist principle of *Wu Wei*—acting without force, flowing naturally with the rhythm of existence.

All the planetary anchors discussed earlier represent fundamental forces of the universe, each powerful in its own way. However, the Sun is the source of all these forces. Just as the planets orbit the Sun, so do all spiritual principles emanate from and return to divine consciousness. When we meditate with the Sun as our anchor, we are not tethering our awareness to a single aspect of reality but to the very foundation of existence itself.

Unlike the planetary anchors, which provide insight into different dimensions of being, the Sun offers direct realization. It is the path of surrender, where there is nothing left to analyze, nothing left to attain—only the simple, ever-present awareness of divine love and light.

This is why, in many mystical traditions, the final step in spiritual practice is not learning but unlearning—not seeking but surrendering. The Sun, as an anchor, teaches us to let go of all other anchors, to dissolve into the presence that has always been with us, waiting for our recognition.

Just as the physical Sun sustains life on Earth, so too does divine consciousness sustain our existence. By meditating on this ultimate reality, we attune ourselves to the deepest truths of our being, allowing ourselves to be illuminated, guided, and ultimately, transformed.

*

They called it the silent dome.

A half-sphere of stone and sky, resting alone on a high plateau where the wind spoke in ancient tongues and clouds moved like slow, thoughtful beasts. There were no roads to it. No paths. Only those who were ready ever found their way there.

Leah had walked all night.

Not because the journey required it, but because something in her had asked for the stars to bear witness. And now, with the first light bleeding across the horizon, she stood before the dome's open arch, breath slow, body stilled by reverence more than exhaustion.

Inside, the air was different. Not heavier. Not lighter. Just— aware. As though the space itself watched gently, inviting without question.

The floor was bare stone, polished smooth by the passing of countless feet. At the center, a circle of gold embedded in the stone radiated a gentle warmth—not physical, but felt in the heart. It pulsed, not with heat, but presence.

She knew she was not alone.

No voices came. No beings appeared. But everything around her—air, silence, light—held a single, resounding truth:

You have arrived.

Leah stepped into the center and sat, legs crossed, spine aligned not with discipline, but with surrender.

She closed her eyes.

There were no mantras. No visualizations. No inner maps to follow.

She had spent years meditating on the planets—on space, life, time, death. She had navigated forces, spirits, fates, and memories. Each had revealed its domain, each had sharpened her awareness.

But this—this was not refinement.

This was the source.

The Sun was not an object of focus now. It was not the fire above. It was the light within.

It had always been there.

She did not descend into meditation.

She was drawn—gently, but completely—into a vast silence that was not empty, but complete.

There, in that stillness, warmth gathered in her chest. Not like heat from fire, but like the remembrance of something sacred. Something true.

It expanded slowly, radiating outward.

She felt it move through her body—not with force, but with grace.

And as it did, her thoughts softened, not from quiet, but from irrelevance.

She was not escaping herself.

She was becoming what she had always been beneath all thought.

The warmth became light.

Not light as she had ever known it—not seen, but recognized.

It filled her, then exceeded her, until there was no border between self and space. She was not bathed in light. She was the light. Not illuminated, but illuminating.

A single phrase emerged—not as sound, but as understanding:

I Am.

And it was enough.

Time unraveled.

There was no sequence. No past arriving into present. No present projecting toward future.

There was only presence.

She felt herself in every moment she had ever lived.

Not remembering. Being.

The child who first saw sunlight flickering through trees.

The young woman crying at the edge of a mistake.

The future self, hands aged but steady, smiling beneath the same stars that had guided her here.

All of them were here.

One flame.

One radiance.

In that unity, fear had no ground.

There was nothing left to defend.

Nothing left to reach.

Only what was.

For a moment—or eternity—she hovered in that sunlit silence, where no prayer was needed because every breath was prayer.

Where love was not emotion but essence.

Where life was not duration, but expression.

And then, gently, she returned.

The dome was unchanged.

The wind passed softly through the arch.

But the world itself now shimmered with meaning.

She stood, not to leave, but to move forward—as if the Sun had stepped into form, and now walked through her bones, her breath, her eyes.

Everything felt clearer.

Not lighter, but more real.

The stone beneath her feet sang its age. The birds in the distance called not as background noise but as fellow voices in the same choir.

And within her, a silence remained—not absence, but fullness.

A flame that could not flicker.

She did not seek visions.

She did not need reassurance.

She had touched what does not change.

And it had touched her back.

As she passed through the arch, she felt no need to look behind.

The Sun was with her now—in every direction, in every shadow.

She descended the pathless plateau.

Not with urgency.

But with light in her step.

Because now she understood:

The Sun does not rise.

It is always here.

Waiting, not to be worshipped.

But to be remembered.

And in that remembrance,

Everything becomes light.

CONCLUSION

The meditation techniques presented in this guide form a comprehensive and holistic system for inner development—one that not only offers a path toward the highest spiritual realization accessible to us as human beings, but also serves as a living reminder that true practice does not end when we rise from our cushion. Rather, meditation is an invitation to dissolve the illusion of separation between formal practice and the rest of our lives. The breath we focus on during stillness is the same breath we carry through every moment of the day. The clarity we cultivate while sitting must be extended into action, speech, and thought. In this way, meditation does not remain confined to a specific posture, time, or place—it permeates everything.

It is natural to regard meditation as a practice distinct from everyday living. We carve out quiet space and structured time, believing that it is during those sacred moments that we step into our true selves. And while formal meditation is indeed essential—a crucible for inner transformation, refinement, and depth—it is only one part of the greater journey. If the wisdom we uncover on the cushion fails to influence how we speak to a friend in distress, respond to a stranger's anger, or engage in the mundane tasks of daily life, then its impact remains partial. The real fruit of meditation is revealed not only in stillness, but in movement—in the echo of patience when hurried, in kindness when provoked, in conscious breath when life becomes overwhelming.

Every emotion we encounter—anger, fear, joy, sadness—is not an interruption to our spiritual journey, but a doorway into it. These emotional currents offer opportunities for integration and awareness. When stress rises or confusion clouds our clarity, the techniques you've learned—diaphragmatic breathing, elemental awareness, observation of sensation, non-reactive witnessing—are not meant to be stored away until your next meditation session. They are tools for life. And life, in all its unpredictability and beauty, becomes the temple in which these tools are forged, tested, and refined.

In time, the border between meditation and life begins to dissolve. The quiet breath you followed during the early morning stillness finds its rhythm again in the middle of a conversation, or while walking through a noisy street, or while lying awake at night. Awareness becomes less something we "do" and more something we inhabit. The reactive mind softens, replaced by presence. Attention no longer clings to every impulse; instead, it rests, moment by moment, where it naturally belongs: in the now.

This integration does not mean that we abandon formal practice. On the contrary, the time spent in silence and stillness becomes more precious than ever. It is during these intentional moments of withdrawal from the noise of the world that we recalibrate, return, and root ourselves more deeply in our essence. Meditation remains the heart of the practice, but not the whole body. It is the wellspring that nourishes every thought, action, and word.

To truly embody the teachings in this book is to understand that spirituality is not a special condition reserved for the meditation hall or the mountaintop. It is just as present in the way we rise from bed in the morning, in the pauses between our words, in the way we touch another person's life—however briefly. It is in the acceptance of each moment as it is, without resistance or clinging. In this way, spiritual life becomes not an escape from the world, but a deeper participation in it.

We are called to view life itself as a continuum of meditative experience—an unbroken thread of presence that stretches from waking to sleeping, from solitude to social engagement, from joy to sorrow. Whether we are sitting in silence, standing in line, or speaking to a loved one, we are given the opportunity to return to ourselves and commune with the deeper intelligence that breathes through us. This is how we come into alignment with our spirit, and, for those who are so inclined, with the divine source that animates all of existence.

Your human experience—brief, intense, beautiful—is not an obstacle to spirituality; it is its vehicle. Let each moment remind you of the sacred. Let each breath bring you home. Let your life be the practice.

Thank you for walking this path. May the insights and methods within this book serve as steady companions on your journey. And may peace, wisdom, and blessings overflow into every part of your life—and into the lives of all you touch.

Printed in Dunstable, United Kingdom